'Within these pages Shaun [...] Christian mindfulness to h [...] the prophetic in our lives. A must-read for all those who are committed to becoming more mindful of God, whilst seeking to grow in the things of the Kingdom.'
Lindsay Melluish, pastor, speaker, therapist, author

'Shaun Lambert's writing and teaching has revolutionised my prayer life. In Putting on the Wakeful One, he reveals the power of the gospel practice of watchfulness. Shaun helps us to awaken fully to the presence of the Holy Spirit in our lives, restoring prayer from labour to joy.'
Rev Will Van Der Hart, Pastoral Chaplain, Holy Trinity Brompton

Putting On the Wakeful One

Attuning to the Spirit of Jesus through watchfulness

Shaun Lambert

instant
apostle

First published in Great Britain in 2016.

Instant Apostle
The Barn
1 Watford House Lane
Watford
Herts
WD17 1BJ

British Library Cataloguing-in-Publication Data

A catalogue record for this book is available from the British Library

This book and all other Instant Apostle books are available from Instant Apostle:

Website: www.instantapostle.com

E-mail: info@instantapostle.com

ISBN 978-1-909728-46-2

Printed in Great Britain

Instant Apostle is a way of getting ideas flowing, between followers of Jesus, and between those who would like to know more about His kingdom.

It's not just about books and it's not about a one-way information flow. It's about building a community where ideas are exchanged. Ideas will be expressed at an appropriate length. Some will take the form of books. But in many cases ideas can be expressed more briefly than in a book. Short books, or pamphlets, will be an important part of what we provide. As with pamphlets of old, these are likely to be opinionated, and produced quickly so that the community can discuss them.

Well-known authors are welcome, but we also welcome new writers. We are looking for prophetic voices, authentic and original ideas, produced at any length; quick and relevant, insightful and opinionated. And as the name implies, these will be released very quickly, either as Kindle books or printed texts or both.

Join the community. Get reading, get writing and get discussing!

'The Wakeful One came down to wake us up
from being submerged in sin.'

Ephrem the Syrian Nativity 1:61-62
quoted in Sebastian Brock's *The Luminous Eye* (141).

Acknowledgements and dedication

God is kind and gracious enough to send us those we need who are encouragers.

Over the last few years John Coles, who is a spiritual *abba* to many people, has been a great encouragement.

Steve Motyer, my supervisor at London School of Theology, is someone who unfailingly sharpens my thinking.

The monks at Worth Abbey have offered a contemplative home and silence in which to listen to God, and a library full of treasure.

I have been at Stanmore Baptist Church for nearly 20 years, and the congregation have embraced change, stability and listening obedience to God, and been a home to my family. It has been a particular joy to work with Joel and Becky Botham (and Patch the dog) over the last few years.

Nicki Copeland has beautifully copy-edited various manuscripts.

This book is dedicated to my wife, Clare, with whom I celebrate our twenty-fifth wedding anniversary this year. Without her I would not have Zac and Amy, our children, or Coco the dog, who is the family timekeeper.

We would both like to also dedicate this book to Rita Jourdan (1929–2015) who treated Clare like a daughter and me like a son, and scattered the gold and silver of the kingdom wherever she walked on earth.

About the author

Shaun Lambert is a Baptist minister in Stanmore, north-west London. He is part of the New Wine leaders' network, and PREMIER Mind and Soul network.

For more than ten years he studied Integrative and Relational Counselling at Roehampton University. He writes regularly for the *Baptist Times* and other Christian publications. He believes that watchfulness and the cultivation of prophetic imagination are central to our transformation as Christians.

Shaun is currently researching a PhD in Practical Theology focusing on watchfulness in Mark's gospel and its relation to secular mindfulness.

He is married to Clare and has two children, Zachary and Amy, and a dog called Coco.

Shaun Lambert is the Senior Minister of Stanmore Baptist Church, Abercorn Road, Stanmore, Middx, HA7 2PH. He can be contacted by email on shaun@stanmorebc.co.uk. You can visit his website at http://shaunlambert.co.uk/.

Contents

Foreword

This readable and accessible book offers a new perspective on discipleship and our own maturity of faith. Using the foundation of studies in mindfulness and associated disciplines, Shaun invites us to intentionally shift our awareness: to become 'watchful' in our faith and to improve our awareness of the physical emotional and spiritual world that is happening all around us.

How can we shift our focus from the culturally obsessed 'self obsession' and the 'gravitational pull' the culture all around us exerts, to instead fix our eyes on God: not just seeing but perceiving with all our senses much more than we would usually be aware of: God's perspective on the world and the people around us. Shaun suggests that we learn to watch in a new way, with a newly 'perceptive faith' and a much wiser understanding of what that means.

Shaun blends information from a fascinating range of backgrounds: psychology, literature and theology to explain and illuminate his concepts and produces a really refreshing read. He introduces new practices of reading, contemplating and meditating on scripture, and encourages the reader to take time not just to read the book but to develop these skills. As such it is a book to take time over: not just to gulp down but to contemplate, digest and dip back into over a period of time. The book can also be read as a series of short studies ideal for small groups, and Shaun has recorded study guides suggesting a format for meetings or discussions as well as a series of podcasts to accompany each section.

The book is a fascinating 'pause for thought' in a busy world: an invitation to open our minds and attentions to what is going on all around us. But perhaps more importantly not only does it offer the chance to change ourselves, but through that change to enable us to be more aware of God's call: not just the big things but the quieter moments, the spiritual nudges: the 'still small voice' that may whisper words of prophecy, encouragement or revelation into the eyes of others.

Dr Kate Middleton, psychologist and church leader, Director of Mind & Soul

Introduction: Putting on the Wakeful One

God as Creator planted a seed of wakefulness in me as a child growing up in Kenya, in what seemed to be a Garden of Eden. Back in England at boarding school I would dream of returning to paradise in East Africa, and as I lay sleeping in the cold I would be suffused with the warmth of a wakeful joy.

I would also dream about travelling on a red murram road, the tyres humming on the soft surface, with the sense that home was just round the corner. I still remember the intense longing to arrive.

It was an inchoate understanding that the focused attention of the thorn trees, the open awareness of the plains and the ground of the animals pointed to something transcendent. The seed lay like a small fragment of light within my heart. It was the uncreated light of being in the presence of Jesus that woke me up. He took off the seed coat of sleep that had been slipped over that little light bulb by a Western culture focused on rational critical thinking and living in the head.

But as I look now at Jesus of Nazareth with a wide-angle lens, I see that He is not just Saviour, central though that is; He is seer and sage, storyteller and transformer of our physical and spiritual senses. This transformative work, which is part of the work of the Holy Spirit in us, enables us to reperceive the world and the kingdom of God at work in it.

These aspects of Jesus' life and ministry have an important role not just in our witness, but also in our transformation. In these roles Jesus could be described, as Ephrem the Syrian poetically puts it, as 'The Wakeful One'.[1] We are to 'put on the Wakeful One' (Jesus) in our baptism.[2] As we put on the Wakeful One, we ourselves can become wakeful, or watchful.

There are key scriptural verses that link to this idea. In 1 Corinthians 2:16 Paul says, 'for, "Who has known the mind of the Lord so as to instruct him?" But we have the mind of Christ.'

In Ephesians 5:14 Paul also says, 'This is why it is said: "Wake up, sleeper, rise from the dead, and Christ will shine on you."'

Romans 13:14, in the context of a call to wake up from sleep (13:11) says, 'Rather, clothe yourselves with the Lord Jesus Christ, and do not think about how to gratify the desires of the flesh.'

When we put on the Wakeful One we put on the mind of Christ; we are waking up from sleep; we are clothing ourselves with the Lord Jesus Christ. What that looks like in terms of our character, which has to be developed alongside prophetic insight, is described in Colossians 3:12: 'clothe yourselves with compassion, kindness, humility, gentleness and patience.'

I believe these verses lie at the heart of what it means to be a disciple, especially the need to wake up and clothe ourselves with Christ. Yet watchfulness seems to have dropped off the horizon of modern discipleship.

---

[1] Sebastian Brock, *The Luminous Eye: The Spiritual World Vision of Saint Ephrem the Syrian* (Kalamazoo, Michigan: Cistercian Publications, 1985), 141.

[2] Brock, *The Luminous Eye*, 141.

When we put on the mind of Christ, what is happening? We work on developing wisdom. We grow in prophetic insight. Through our salvation in Jesus Christ we indwell the Great Story of the gospel. Our spiritual and embodied senses are transformed, enabling us to reperceive the world. As all this happens we are transformed into the likeness of Jesus, the Wakeful One. As we clothe ourselves with Him, we become more compassionate, kind, humble, gentle and patient. We move from a place of fear and blindness to a place of love and truth. All this is the work of God's Holy Spirit within us who leads us to Christ, as Christ leads us to the Father.

These different aspects of discipleship are ripe for a fresh look and a recontextualisation in our postmodern world that is looking anew at spirituality, wisdom and reading the signs of the times. As the church, one of our central tasks is to read aright the signs of the times.

Part of watchfulness

These aspects which I am summarising are all part of 'watchfulness' as modelled and taught by Jesus. They help us establish a clearer view on the making of prophecy and the maturing of the prophetic, which is the central theme of this book. The prophetic here is seen in a wider and more holistic sense than is often portrayed. Prophetic insight is all to do with attention and awareness, and so this is the major part of what this book concentrates on. *Jesus and watchfulness is where we begin in chapter one.* In watchfulness we are attuning ourselves to the Spirit of Jesus.

Part of this re-evaluation comes out of developments in biblical scholarship which recognise that the gospel is an embodied gospel. Natural and incarnational theology enable us to re-envision prophecy as something that is done incarnationally using the God-given senses and capacities that

17

we inhabit our bodies with, enabling them to be spiritually attuned to the hidden kingdom which is part of the one reality we inhabit.[3]

A rediscovery of attention and awareness within psychology, in particular through the research of cognitive neuroscience, should also alert us to the focus of the gospels and the early church on the importance of watchfulness.

Where are the mature prophets?

Another central reason for writing this book was in response to a question raised by one of the founders of the New Wine festivals, Barry Kissell, who asked, 'Where are the mature prophets?'[4] This is not to say that there are not those around who are mature in working with the prophetic, but I do think a clear and consistent model of developing it as an every-member ministry, as part of a broader discipleship, is very much needed today.

In order to enable the maturing of prophecy we need to look again at how it is made, as a co-created process between God's Spirit and Word and the human being willing to be attentive in such a process.

As Peter reminds us in 2 Peter 1:21, 'For prophecy never had its origin in the human will, but prophets, though human, spoke from God as they were carried along by the Holy Spirit.' The prophets were never robots: they worked with the Holy Spirit, and God used their individual personalities and gifts.

John Robinson, one of the early Baptists, said, 'The Lord hath more truth and light yet to break forth from His holy

---

[3] For example see Joel B. Green, 'Embodying the Gospel: Two Examplary Practices', *Journal of Spiritual Formation & Soul Care* 7, no. 1 (2014).

[4] This was probably at a New Wine summer conference but I cannot place which one.

word.'[5] There are many things that each culture misses in Scripture that have become blind spots, or have fallen off the radar. Watchfulness is one of them in the modern church. But there are interesting aspects about prophecy that have also been missed. There has been some important research done on the types of prophecy embedded in the New Testament that can help us discern what is real when it comes to the prophetic and what is not.[6]

Mark's gospel is an oral gospel, which would have been performed, proclaimed in its entirety, from beginning to end. It has a lot to say about watchfulness, both explicitly and implicitly. Another reason for writing this book is to encourage Christians to read Mark's gospel in new ways and to listen to it as a whole. As we look at the different elements that will make up our focus, I will be sharing other ways that we can productively read Mark's gospel.

Each chapter will include a passage from the gospel for you to read slowly and meditatively. I also encourage you to listen to one of the performances of Mark's gospel as a whole.[7] In particular throughout the book, but also in the spiritual practices I expand on at the end, I want to ask the question, 'Yes, but how?'

---

[5] Encyclopaedia Britannica, 'John Robinson, English minister'. Available at http://www.britannica.com/biography/John-Robinson-English-minister (accessed 16th November 2015).

[6] David E. Aune, *Prophecy in Early Christianity and the Ancient Mediterranean World* (Grand Rapids, Michigan: William B. Eerdmans Publishing Company, 1983).

[7] My favourite is a performance by Max McLean which you can buy online or watch online:
https://www.youtube.com/watch?v=td3FKGN1AsM (accessed 16th November 2015).

Immersing in Scripture

To further briefly introduce this important element of the book, as well as listening to the whole of Mark's gospel in audio form or as a performance, I would urge you to immerse yourself in the rest of Scripture in audio form as well.[8] Each day, stay with one passage or verse. Our example here should be the psalmist.

What is a psalm? Have a think about that for a moment without reading on.

Psalm 1 gives us our clue:

> Blessed is the one
> who does not walk in step with the wicked
> or stand in the way that sinners take
> or sit in the company of mockers,
> but whose delight is in the law of the Lord,
> and who *meditates* on his law day and night.
> *Psalm 1:1-2 (italics added)*

The psalms are not ordered randomly, and Psalm 1 is placed especially at the beginning to highlight the importance of meditation in the creation of the psalms.[9]

Psalm 19 spells this out even more clearly in the last verse of the psalm (verse 14): 'May these words of my mouth and *this meditation of my heart* be pleasing in your sight, Lord, my Rock and my Redeemer' (italics added). As William P. Brown puts it, 'The last verse marks the entire psalm as the speaker's

---

[8] Here is a good link giving you some options, http://www.premierchristianity.com/Past-Issues/2015/November-2015/Bible-Tech (accessed 16th November 2015).

[9] William P. Brown, *Psalms* (Nashville, Abingdon Press, 2010), 82.

discourse ("meditation") of both the "mouth" and "heart" offered to YHWH.'[10]

To apply this to Psalm 1, the psalmist meditates on God's Word, and the psalm is the fruit of his meditation – i.e., it is itself a meditation. This means we ourselves can use the psalm to meditate.

What does this meditation look like? It is an immersion ('day and night'); it is repetitive: if you are meditating day and night on a passage you are not just looking at it once.

In so doing, the psalmist exercises the muscle of attention, not only in what he is focusing on, but also in the actual creation of the psalm. The psalm is not a casual collection of words, but is carefully crafted.

When exercising the muscle of attention, focusing our attention on, for example, 'the law of the Lord', our minds will wander. We notice what our mind has wandered to, and direct it back to Scripture. As we do this and enter a place of stillness (Psalm 46:10), we become more openly aware of the presence of God and are able to listen to the prophetic insights He wishes to share.

The psalmists developed this attentive way of looking at reality (the world in which we live and the hidden kingdom within it) through the lens of Scripture, which enabled them to meditate on nature and see it as creation:

> When I *consider* your heavens,
> the work of your fingers,
> the moon and the stars,
> which you have set in place,
> what is mankind that you are mindful of them,
> human beings that you care for them?
> *Psalm 8:3-4 (italics added)*

---

[10] Brown, *Psalms*, 83.

'Consider' is a meditative word, and through this meditation the psalmist receives a prophetic insight that God is 'mindful' of humanity. That means God remembers humanity with loving attention that results in Him reaching out towards us.

Understandably, the church has majored on Jesus as Saviour, but often in a reductionist and truncated manner. *We can look at Jesus as Saviour in Mark's gospel in a watchful way*, and I will do this in chapter two. Scripture tells us that none of us sees or hears clearly; we have distorted perceptive faculties including spiritual and ethical ones – this is part of the Fall. This means that salvation also involves restoring our ability to see clearly at a spiritual, ethical and relational level. Paul spells this out in Acts 26:17-18 when he declares what God has said is his calling as an apostle: 'I am sending you to them to open their eyes and turn them from darkness to light...' One of the central aspects of human sinfulness is that we think we see clearly when we don't. This is very clear in Mark's gospel, where the disciples consistently fail to see clearly. When we are saved, we are saved from blindness, and from the pride that believes we are not blind. There are, of course, many other aspects of salvation, but I want to bring this aspect from the backstage onto the frontstage.

To enable us to appreciate this aspect of salvation I will then say something about the *attentional capacities* we use. I have already touched on this, but I will explore it in more depth in the body of the book.

Out of this I will explore in more depth the idea of *Jesus and the senses*. This is one of those hidden elements in Scripture, from which new light needs to break forth. More recent scholarship recognises that the gospel is an embodied gospel. As Alister McGrath says, 'It is merely to assert that for human beings in this world the transcendent is accessed and the spiritual life is expressed exclusively through the medium of our material bodies.'[11]

Recognising this will rescue us from being over-spiritual, and from the Gnostic heresy that riddles the church – that the body is bad and the spirit is good. This is a false dualism which is not part of the Hebrew mindset of the Old Testament or the way Jesus lived and spoke in the New Testament. To assist us, we will look at what the cognitive neuroscience of attention and awareness says about our God-given attentional capacities at work in watchfulness.

When we look at the gospels, we also see *Jesus as Seer*. Again, this is often a neglected part of our witness and discipleship, almost as if in a reductionist, materialistic culture we are ashamed of Jesus and His supernatural insight. Our culture is changing, and we can now shine a light on this important part of who Jesus is. That means we too, as followers of Christ, are to cultivate prophetic insight and read the signs of the times. I think this can be interpreted much more widely than is often the case in charismatic subcultures within the church.

What is also illuminating about looking at Jesus in the gospels is to see *Jesus as Sage*. Wisdom as a construct is being re-examined by modern psychology, and ancient forms of wisdom, such as mindfulness, are being explored and recontextualised. As Christians we live in a culture where wisdom has been swamped by an information overload, and a quest for knowledge without wisdom. We need to put wisdom back in our repertoire of virtues to cultivate.

It is generally recognised that Jesus is a *Storyteller*, but these stories, parables and riddles are used by Jesus in His capacity as Seer, Sage and Saviour and hence can help show what it

---

[11] Alister E. McGrath, *The Open Secret: A New Vision for Natural Theology* (Oxford, Blackwell Publishing, 2008), 82.

means to become prophetically insightful, watchful, wise and saved. Parables are like flowers, to be contemplated, but we pick them to pieces and examine each petal as if in that act the parable is not destroyed, as the flower is destroyed. Parables are to help us reperceive the world, and perceive the kingdom of God in the world.

It would help us to apply all this learning to see how the *Desert Sages and Seers* of the early church took up Jesus' teaching on watchfulness, and became discerners of the signs of their times.

These two chapters will enable me to address the important questions: How do I become watchful and discern the signs of the times? How do I become mature in the prophetic? Like Jesus, and like the Desert Sages and Seers, we need to become contemplatives and practise contemplation.

In the later chapters of the book we will explore two contemplative practices in particular. The first is *Lectio Divina*, a slow meditative reading of Scripture that helps develop our watchfulness and prophetic insight. The second is the Jesus Prayer, an ancient Christian prayer: 'Lord Jesus Christ, Son of God, have mercy on me, a sinner.' It is an embodied prayer that uses our breath and brings us into a contemplative state of mind.

Finally, if we are to read the signs of the times for our own age, what might we see?

Intention, attention and attitude

To answer the question, 'How do I mature in prophetic insight and watchfulness?' I would ask you as the reader to work on three key things: intention, attention and attitude.

These key transformational practices are part of biblical and contemplative tradition. These practices are also being highlighted in secular psychology, especially in the area of mindfulness.

How might we define mindfulness? The most well-known definition is by Jon Kabat-Zinn: 'Mindfulness means paying attention in a particular way: on purpose, in the present moment, and nonjudgmentally.'[12] This definition can be broken down into three main components: of intention, attention and attitude.[13]

Intention is very important. For example, I use secular mindful awareness practices to face my anxiety. I use Christian mindful awareness practices to come into the presence of God, in whose love my fear dissolves. Jesus put intention at the heart of the attentive life: 'But *seek* first his kingdom and his righteousness, and all these things will be given to you as well' (Matthew 6:33, italics added). Out of our intention comes the motivation to keep seeking, to keep meditating. Bernard of Clairvaux also put *intentio*, intention, at the heart of the life of prayer. At the heart of *intentio* is the idea of looking closely at God with what Bernard called 'the face of the soul'.[14]

The second key element of mindfulness is attention, which is how we use our awareness. Awareness is 'attending to

---

[12] Jon Kabat-Zinn, *Wherever You Go, There You Are: Mindfulness Meditation in Everyday Life* (New York: Hyperion, 1994), 4, quoted in Zindel V. Segal, J. Mark G. Williams and John D. Teasdale, *Mindfulness-Based Cognitive Therapy for Depression* (New York: Guilford Press, 2002), 40.
[13] Shauna L. Shapiro et al., 'Mechanisms of Mindfulness', *Journal of Clinical Psychology* 62, no.3 (2006): 374. Available at http://dx.doi.org/10.1002/jclp.20237 (accessed 16th November 2015).
[14] Michael Casey, *Athirst For God: Spiritual Desire in Bernard of Clairvaux's Sermons on the Song of Songs* (Kalamazoo: Cistercian Publications, 1988), 117.

experience itself, as it presents itself in the here and now.'[15] Jesus commands us to clearly focus our attention. He does this through stories where we fail to pay attention to the detail: '*Look* at the birds of the air; they do not sow or reap or store away in barns, and yet your heavenly Father feeds them' (Matthew 6:26, italics added). This is not a casual glance but involves *looking* with attention and awareness for the wisdom embedded in the life of these small birds.

Shapiro et al. suggest that the third axiom of mindfulness is attitude. They argue that we can learn to face reality with acceptance, kindness and openness, seeing clearly what is there.[16] Very importantly, they say that this enables us to develop 'the capacity not to continually strive for pleasant experiences, or to push aversive experiences away.'[17]

Jesus tells us to face the reality of our internal attitudes: 'Why do you look at the speck of sawdust in your brother's eye and pay no attention to the plank in your own eye?' (Matthew 7:3). He also commands us to be non-judgemental and to practise being non-judgemental in a continuous way: 'Do not judge, or you too will be judged' (Matthew 7:1). What He commends is clear seeing: 'First take the plank out of your own eye, and then you will see clearly to remove the speck from your brother's eye' (Matthew 7:5).

So we will be using the following outline in this book:

- Introduction – Putting on the Wakeful One
- Jesus and watchfulness
- Jesus as Saviour
- The attentional capacities we use

---

[15] Shapiro et al., 'Mechanisms of Mindfulness', 376.
[16] Shapiro et al., 'Mechanisms of Mindfulness', 377.
[17] Shapiro et al., 'Mechanisms of Mindfulness', 377.

- Jesus and the senses – the embodied gospel

- Jesus as Seer

- Jesus as Sage

- Jesus as Storyteller

- The Desert Sages and Seers and watchfulness

- Becoming watchful through Scripture

- Becoming watchful through contemplation

- Reading the signs of these times

Each chapter will have a short opportunity at the end to reflect on what you have read. In particular, I will be trying to encourage you to think about these three transformative aspects of intention, attention and awareness.

Try to read slowly and with awareness, exercising your muscle of attention (see the section 'Using the muscle of attention' in chapter 9). I suggest you read just two chapters a week, and take seriously the suggested passages for *Lectio Divina*. You can also practise the Jesus Prayer every day.

There is a study guide at the end, which you can use whether you are reading the book alone or in a small group.

Chapter one
Jesus and watchfulness

The origin of the word 'watchfulness'

The idea of 'watchfulness' has its roots in the wisdom and prophetic books of the Old Testament. It appears in Mark's gospel in particular as an idea and is represented by different words, both implicitly and explicitly. Reading Mark's gospel in the light of the influence of Judaism, Marie Noonan Sabin makes the helpful point that Jesus' command to be watchful (Mark 13:37) is an instruction 'about the ongoing need to respond to God's presence.'[18] Prophetic insight in all its fullness requires a watchfulness for, and an awareness of, God's presence. This awareness can be cultivated. We can talk about the Word as a seed as Jesus does, which grows inside us as the seed of the kingdom (Mark 4:1-9). This seed includes the fruit of prophetic insight within it, as well as all the fullness of being clothed with Jesus, of being Spirit-bearers and those who enter and receive the kingdom of God.

Have a look now at the section on *Lectio Divina* in chapter 9. *Lectio Divina* is a slow meditative reading of Scripture that develops our watchfulness and enables us to listen to God. Then take the Garden of Gethsemane account (Mark 14:32-42)

---

[18] Marie Noonan Sabin, *Reopening the Word: Reading Mark as Theology in the Context of Early Judaism* (Oxford: Oxford University Press, 2002), 72.

and read it in this slow, attentive way, before reading the rest of the chapter. Stay with the passage all day, and come back to it at regular intervals.

Watchfulness and the Garden of Gethsemane

It is very important to begin with the scriptural evidence, and watchfulness in the Garden of Gethsemane is the beating heart of the theme in Mark's gospel. What we need to realise, though, is that we won't understand what this passage says if we take it in isolation. Deep veins run into this passage from earlier in the gospel which illuminate watchfulness within the garden, and deep veins run out from the passage into the final chapters, shedding further light on the landscape of watchfulness that runs throughout the gospel.

Mark's gospel is one story made up of smaller stories linked together by the repetition of key words, and the use of verbal threads and other stylistic devices.

If we take the thread of 'watchfulness', Mark shows us different ways of watching, along with the way(s) of watching that Jesus' commands and commends. The verbal thread begins back in Mark 3, where Jesus is in a synagogue and a man with a shrivelled hand is there. Some teachers of the law look to accuse Jesus, 'so they watched him closely to see if he would heal him on the Sabbath' (Mark 3:2).

This suspicious form of watching – judgemental and accusing – is not what Jesus models for us.

Our culture is increasingly dominated by a self-focused attention that centres on anxious preoccupation with self and rumination, to the detriment of our mental health.[19] Jesus

---

[19] Mark A. Lau et al., 'The Toronto Mindfulness Scale: Development and Validation', *Journal of Clinical Psychology* 62, no. 12 (2006), 1447. Available at http://dx.doi.org/10.1002/jclp.20326 (accessed 16th November 2015).

warns against this self-focused anxious and fearful attention, when He says in Mark 8:35, 'For whoever wants to save their life will lose it.'

This self-focused attention can be seen in other ways. Jesus, outlining the way of the cross in Mark 8, adds in verse 36, 'What good is it for someone to gain the whole world, yet forfeit their soul?' This acquisitive watching is another way we are shaped in the patterns of this world (Romans 12:2).

Jesus gives us one more example of self-focused attention. Three times in Mark's gospel He prophesies about His suffering on the cross, His death and His resurrection (8:31-32; 9:30-32; 10:32-34). The second time, in chapter 9, the disciples have just been arguing about who is the greatest (9:34). This competitive watching is contrary to the values of the gospel, as Jesus will lay out in His teaching. This is where the gospel challenges our *attitudes* (fearful, acquisitive and competitive), invites us *intentionally* to shift our attitude, and commands us to work on our *attention* and awareness.

The watchfulness Jesus commands and models for us has both a negative aspect and a positive aspect. I have outlined some of the ways of watching we learn as patterns of this world. But now we need to turn to what Jesus models for us. This is where we cannot view themes or passages in isolation. Another central theme that runs through the gospel, characterised by verbal threads and other stylistic devices, is that of 'the Way'.

Watchfulness and the Way

Christians were called followers of 'the Way' (Acts 9:2) before they were called Christians. Mark's gospel begins with John the Baptist preparing the way for the Lord (1:1-8). The followers of Jesus are also expected in the gospel to be on the Way, following the ethical path of the kingdom as laid out by

Jesus. Again, this would have echoes from the Old Testament: 'You shall walk in all the way which the Lord your God has commanded you' (Deuteronomy 5:33, NASB).

In this sense of an ethical path, the repetitions and verbal threads that lay out the 'Way' of the cross can be traced throughout Mark's gospel, although we wouldn't pick it up in most translations as they tend to translate words that reoccur with a range of other words (2:23; 4:4; 4:15; 8:27; 9:33; 9:34; 10:32; 10:46; 10:52, 12:14). These are all variations of the Greek word *hodos*.

Staying on the Way for a follower of Jesus is not easy. This is where the two themes of the Way and watchfulness overlap. Susan R. Garrett calls 'watchfulness' in the Garden of Gethsemane part of the vocabulary of 'eschatological testing' that occurs throughout chapters 13 and 14.[20]

Jesus is tested in the garden, as He looks ahead to the trial of the cross that awaits Him. Does He follow the Way of the cross all the way to His death? Indeed, He prays in Mark 14:35, demonstrating His full humanity (though without sinning), 'that if possible the hour might pass from him'. The *hour* is another word of eschatological testing.[21]

The Garden of Gethsemane and the cross are not the only times of testing, trial and temptation in the gospel for Jesus. At the beginning of the gospel Jesus is tempted (*peirazo*) by Satan in the wilderness. He is tested by the Pharisees. In Mark 8:11 we read, 'The Pharisees came and began to question Jesus. To test him, they asked him for a sign from heaven.'[22]

---

[20] Susan R. Garrett, *The Temptations of Jesus in Mark's Gospel* (Grand Rapids, Michigan: William B. Eerdmans Publishing Company, 1998), 78.

[21] Garrett, *The Temptations of Jesus in Mark's Gospel*, 92.

[22] Garrett, *The Temptations of Jesus in Mark's Gospel*, 68. For more on this theme, see also Mark 10:2; 12:15.

But the disciples also test Him, in one of the most important exchanges in Mark's gospel. Three times Jesus prophesies about His death on the cross, and each time the disciples are guilty of experiential avoidance: they do not want to know about the way of the cross (Mark 8:34). On the first occasion He talks about His suffering, Peter takes Him aside and rebukes Him (8:32). Jesus in turn rebukes Peter in the hearing of the other disciples, '"Get behind me, Satan!" he said. "You do not have in mind the concerns of God, but merely human concerns"' (Mark 8:33).

It is clear from Jesus' very strong reply to Peter that He is being tempted here, tempted as He is in the Garden to not walk the way of the cross. Throughout the gospel Jesus is faced with many ethical moments of choice, and He is able to choose the concern, or thing, of God in each moment because He is watchful and aware, both of the human concerns jostling for His attention and the things of God. Choosing the things of God in the ethical moment helps us stay on the way of the cross, to stay on the right path.

I would also argue that Jesus here is laying out what He is trying to teach His disciples – that they, in their ethical moments of choice, need to choose the things of God over the human concerns of self-focused attention, whether the saving of self or the acquisition of wealth or power. It is here we see that developing prophetic insight and maturing the prophetic is very much tied in with the development of our character and values, and actually living those out in the moments of our lives.

This is where we can come back to our theme of watchfulness in the Garden of Gethsemane. Jesus is faced with a choice: does He do the thing of God and go to the cross, or does He listen to His very human concerns? And the disciples are also faced with an ethical choice. This choice is less clear, but nonetheless it is there.

This is the negative aspect of the watchfulness Jesus is teaching that helps us stay on the way. One of the questions that can be asked about the passage in the Garden is, 'Why does Jesus take Peter, James and John with Him?'

There is a thread here to trace as well, as this is the third occasion that these three have been with Jesus apart from the other disciples. In Mark 5 when He raises Jairus' daughter from the dead, Jesus takes Peter, James and John with Him (5:37). Here they see the miracles of the kingdom at work through Jesus, a foretaste of the salvation that is on offer through Him.

In Mark 9 when Jesus is transfigured, He again takes Peter, James and John with Him (9:2). Here they see Him revealed in the fullness of His divinity. Finally, in the Garden they are with Him and they see Him in the fullness of His humanity:

> For we do not have a high priest who is unable to feel
> sympathy for our weaknesses, but we have one who
> has been tempted in every way, just as we are – yet
> he did not sin.
> *Hebrews 4:15*

But there is another connection between Peter, James and John: their lack of self-awareness, and the pride that leads them to boast about how they will stay with Jesus to the end. In Mark 10:35-45 James and John ask to sit at Jesus' right and at His left when He comes into His glory. Jesus asks them if they can drink from the cup of suffering He has to drink, and they say in verse 39, 'We can…'

After the Last Supper, and as Jesus takes His disciples out to the Mount of Olives, He prophesies that the disciples will fall away and abandon Him. Peter declares (14:29), 'Even if all fall away, I will not.'

Jesus replies with the famous statement that 'before the cock crows twice you yourself will disown me three times' (14:30).

It could be that Jesus invites Peter, James and John to watch with Him for their sake and not just His, and in particular because of their protestations of loyalty.[23]

In the Garden, Jesus goes off to pray, deeply distressed, having asked the three with Him to keep watch. When He returns He finds them asleep and says, 'Couldn't you keep watch for one hour? Watch and pray so that you will not fall into temptation' (14:37-38).

Who is it that they need to watch, and what is the temptation they will face? It is clear from Jesus' follow-up words, 'The spirit is willing, but the flesh is weak' (Mark 14:38), that Peter, James and John need to watch themselves. They are going to be tested. But in what way are they being tempted? Drawing on R. T. France's commentary on this passage, we see that they have promised loyalty but will be tempted to be disloyal (as indeed they demonstrate once Jesus is arrested – 14:50).[24] This is the negative element of watchfulness that Jesus commands, that we need to watch our sinful inclination to disloyalty.

Commentators generally link the words about watchfulness in the Garden of Gethsemane passage to the idea of eschatological testing because of the parable that precedes it in chapter 13. In this famous parable Jesus talks about His return: 'But about that day or hour no one knows, not even the angels in heaven' (13:32). The disciples are commanded to be watchful in the present because they do not know the future

---

[23] Garrett, *The Temptations of Jesus in Mark's Gospel*, 94.

[24] R. T. France, *The Gospel of Mark:The New International Greek Testament Commentary* (Grand Rapids, Michigan: William B. Eerdmans Publishing Company, 2002), 587.

date of His return. Jesus ends the parable with another admonition, which is for all disciples, in all times and places: 'What I say to you, I say to everyone: "Watch!"' (13:37). This means that the time of eschatological testing, the time of trial signified by the word 'watch', is a time of trial for all Christians. We ourselves live in a time of trial. We also, therefore, need to be watchful, and to learn how to cultivate watchfulness.

Like the disciples, we need to watch ourselves so that we are not tempted to disloyalty, and we need to watch the present for signs of the times, as with Jesus' analogy of the fig tree blossoming (13:28-29).

But there is another side to watchfulness, which is the positive kingdom virtue of looking out for opportunities to be welcoming and hospitable. Jesus shows us how to do this. He was welcoming and hospitable to those who were dismissed as unimportant by the rest of society. We see this with His encounter with some little children (Mark 10:13-16):

> People were bringing little children to Jesus for him to place his hands on them, but the disciples rebuked them. When Jesus saw this, he was indignant. He said to them, 'Let the little children come to me, and do not hinder them, for the kingdom of God belongs to such as these. Truly I tell you, anyone who will not receive the kingdom of God like a little child will never enter it.' And he took the children in his arms, placed his hands on them and blessed them.

If we look at this passage from the perspective of attention and awareness, we see that the disciples have not been attentive to what Jesus has been teaching about the kingdom. To use some words that are about attention and awareness, Jesus is present; He is attuned to the needs of the children and resonates with their wonder and awe.[25] He knows what they want, and here is an embodied response: He takes them in his arms and blesses them. The welcome and hospitality that Jesus shows to those that others reject can be seen many, many times.

I don't know if you have ever experienced the feeling of gratitude when someone unexpectedly digs you out of a hole in an act of grace. What I have also experienced is God's watchful grace. As the Old Testament puts it in Psalm 121:5, 'The Lord watches over you – the Lord is your shade at your right hand.'

There is also the idea of His people being watchmen and women: 'I have posted watchmen on your walls, Jerusalem' (Isaiah 62:6). This idea is taken up in the New Testament with the idea of spiritual warfare and putting on the armour of God in Ephesians 6:10-18, which includes the command to be alert (v.18). Sometimes God's watchful grace towards me has been at night when He has given me warning dreams as I have slept, to help me as the shepherd of His flock in Stanmore.

We need to work with God in cultivating watchfulness, but the gracious way He is mindful of us is remarkable.

---

[25] See Daniel J. Siegel, *The Mindful Therapist* (New York: W. W. Norton & Company, 2010), xx-xxi, for definitions of these concepts and how they lead to trust.

Reflection

Intention

Nothing changes without the intention to change. Make it your intention to take on the spiritual practices of watchfulness.

Attention

Where normally is the focus of your attention?

Attitude

Notice where your attitude is self-focused, fearful, anxious and suspicious. Pray for it to be replaced by love and compassion with truth.

Chapter two
Jesus as Saviour

Introduction

Read Mark 1.

Over nearly 30 years as a Christian I have always been involved with charismatic evangelical churches which seek to follow the twin tracks of the Holy Spirit and God's Word. This has also involved national movements like New Wine, which is principally Anglican but draws in many other denominations.[26] In addition, I have led retreats for a Roman Catholic Benedictine monastery, as well as for Anglican and evangelical retreat organisations.

What I have noticed within charismatic circles is that teaching about prophecy often just focuses on the explicitly biblical strand of teaching on prophecy, without drawing in the context within which that teaching appears. Mark's gospel is a useful analogy. It is generally seen as an oral gospel, and one that was constructed to be listened to as a whole. But what we tend to do is take individual stories and passages and focus on those, and consequently lose the beautiful woven patterns of the whole.

---

[26] See the New Wine website for more details: http://www.new-wine.org/ (accessed 17th November 2015).

Developing the prophetic cannot be addressed apart from being immersed in the rest of Scripture and the requirements of discipleship and being a follower of Jesus. This is why I want to set it in the context of Jesus as Saviour, Sage, Seer and Storyteller, and within natural and incarnational theology which recognises that our spiritual life needs to be earthed in our embodied, relational createdness.

Mark's gospel presents a clear understanding of Jesus as Saviour. There are many other books in the New Testament that add to this picture, but here I am principally focusing on what Mark teaches in his gospel. As your *Lectio* passage for today, read Mark 1:1-20, which introduces Jesus who brings the *saving* rule of the kingdom.

Attending to the gospel

Now with Mark's gospel it is a truism that 'we learn who Jesus is not so much from what he says as from what he does'.[27] I would nuance that to what He says is as important as what He does, but His actions are often important as enacted or embodied parables and prophetic signs. I will say more about that later on.

It is also generally recognised that thematically Mark writes in an implicit way, 'requiring readers to enter into the drama of the gospel in order to understand its meaning'.[28] In this sense the whole gospel could be perceived as being parabolic. I believe this is intentional on the part of Mark, because it requires a different response from the reader and listener. What it requires is a deep attentiveness and open awareness to what God may be saying through the words and actions of

---

[27] James R. Edwards, *The Gospel According to Mark: The Pillar New Testament Commentary* (Leicester: Apollos, 2002), 13.
[28] Edwards, *The Gospel According to Mark*, 13.

Jesus. We have to bear in mind that 'every pericope in Mark is about Jesus except for two about John the Baptizer'.[29]

Jesus' teaching, life and acts in Mark's gospel can be summarised as proclaiming and bringing the kingdom. The kingdom of God (called the kingdom of heaven elsewhere) is the kingdom of salvation and wholeness, the future transformation of humanity and creation breaking into the present.[30]

Jesus and the kingdom

Part of the transformation, salvation and healing that Jesus brings in this way is to enable us to see clearly, to reperceive the world, and to see the mysterious hidden kingdom of God at work in the world.

If we fix our gaze on Jesus then we find the kingdom, because 'in Jesus of Nazareth the kingdom of God makes a personal appearance'.[31] It is 'near', when He is near (Mark 1:15).

In a piece of detail that is often missed as we skim-read Scripture, when Jesus appoints the 12 it is in part 'that they might be with him' (3:14). Part of the transformation that occurs in the disciples, and in all disciples, is when they are in the *presence* of Jesus.[32] In Jesus we come near to the kingdom of

---

[29] Edwards, *The Gospel According to Mark*, 12. A pericope is a technical term used in New Testament scholarship about a passage that can stand alone in analysis in terms of meaning.

[30] Edwards, *The Gospel According to Mark*, 46-47.

[31] Edwards, *The Gospel According to Mark*, 47.

[32] Suzanne Watts Henderson, *Christology and Discipleship in the Gospel of Mark* (Cambridge: Cambridge University Press, 2006), 4.

God. As theologian Hans Kung puts it, 'God's kingdom is creation healed.'[33]

When people were in the presence of Jesus, they received insights, they found faith, they were able to see clearly, as with Bartimaeus (Mark 10:52). In the presence of Jesus people were also inflamed with prophetic and embodied feelings, as in Mark 9:15: 'As soon as all the people saw Jesus, they were overwhelmed with wonder and ran to greet him.' It may be, as we are filled with the presence of Jesus and our prophetic awareness is activated, that we are filled with wonder, awe and reverence, and that this enables other feelings as well. Awe and wonder as feelings are prophetic in this sense because we are recognising, as Jesus' first listeners did, that He is indeed God incarnate. The community can then begin to access insights, faith and clear seeing.

Many times in Mark's gospel, those who meet Jesus are filled with these prophetic feelings, as in Mark 5:42, when Jesus raised the little girl from the dead. When she stood up and walked, 'they were completely astonished'. Literally in the Greek it says 'and they were astonished immediately with a great astonishment'.

Mark also has important things to say about faith, salvation and the kingdom. As can be seen by the miracles listed by Mark, the kingdom of God is 'the present manifestation of God's eschatological power.'[34]The power from the future is breaking into the present. But, as I want to outline throughout this book, the impact of the kingdom in terms of salvation cannot just be narrowed down to getting a 'ticket to heaven',

---

[33] *A Time to Heal – A Report for the House of Bishops on the Healing Ministry* (Church House Publishing, 2007), 25.

[34] Christopher D. Marshall, *Faith as a Theme in Mark's Narrative* (Cambridge: Cambridge University Press, 1989), 232.

to 'pie in the sky when we die', but this power impacts 'all areas of life'.[35]

What we will also unpack, in terms of one of the main strands of our salvation and transformation, is the ability to see clearly, to discern, to read the signs of the times – again in a holistic way, in all areas of life, 'the spiritual and the physical, the ethical and the social, the religious and the political'.[36] We are also to prophetically imagine kingdom futures that are to break into the present as signs of the kingdom.[37]

A perceptive faith

Christopher Marshall is particularly helpful here because he outlines that the faith we are called to in Mark's gospel by Jesus is *perceptive* faith: 'it is because the attitude of perceptive dependence – which is Markan faith – is alone capable of receiving Jesus' deeds as revelatory acts of God.'[38]

What lies at the heart of perceptive faith? Watchfulness lies at the heart of perceptive faith. Even with our fallen nature we have a natural capacity to be watchful, but it needs to be redeemed and transformed by the grace and power of God. Perceptive faith seeks the way like water, like light.

It is also true in Mark's gospel that alongside the repetitions and verbal threads are key concepts and verses that are significant because they only appear once or a few times. That doesn't mean they are not important: it means they *are* important.

---

[35] Marshall, *Faith as a Theme in Mark's Narrative*, 232.

[36] Marshall, *Faith as a Theme in Mark's Narrative*, 232.

[37] See Walter Brueggeman, *The Prophetic Imagination*, second edition (Minneapolis: Fortress Press, 2001).

[38] Marshall, *Faith as a Theme in Mark's Narrative*, 234.

For example, a key summary verse is Mark 10:45, where Jesus says, 'For even the Son of Man did not come to be served, but to serve, and to give his life as a ransom for many.'

Although this is one of the few explicit statements of Jesus in His role as Saviour in Mark's gospel, actually all His prior actions and teaching lead to this verse, and everything He does afterwards leads from this verse. So if you were reading just explicit statements out of context, you could miss how central this idea is to Mark's gospel.

Giving and serving, which lies at the heart of this verse, is 'authoritative for and transferable to disciples'.[39] However, Jesus, and Jesus alone, can give His life as a ransom for many.

I think there has been a movement among Christians to decide that learning Greek, the original language of the New Testament, is too difficult. However, if we make the effort to engage with it in our devotional reading and Bible study, it can open the door to a greater love, understanding and indwelling of Scripture.

This comes out in Mark 10:45 if we look at some of the key words in the Greek. One of those words is *lytron*, translated 'ransom', which carries some key ideas around salvation. The first is about freedom, setting us free from slavery. As C. Clifton Black puts it in his commentary on Mark's gospel, 'In Mark the Son of Man does not present himself as a new master; he is, instead, the release of others from slavery.'[40]

This freedom is experienced here on earth as well as in heaven. It is a spiritual freedom that brings with it embodied, psychological and cultural freedom. It moves us from a place of fear and self-focused attention to a place where we can give to and serve others in the way that Jesus does.

---

[39] Edwards, *The Gospel According to Mark*, 326.
[40] C. Clifton Black, *Mark: Abingdon New Testament Commentaries* (Nashville: Abingdon Press, 2011), 233.

The key thing to understand is that we cannot free ourselves; there is no ransom we ourselves can pay to release us out of our bondage.

Another important reason for loving the original Greek of the New Testament is that in Mark there are many allusions and echoes to the Greek version of the Old Testament, the Septuagint. In Mark 10:45 there are references and verbal echoes to Isaiah 53, in particular the idea of 'voluntarily giving up life'.[41] This life 'is offered as a substitute for their guilt', the guilt of the many (meaning all).[42]

In the word *lytron* (ransom) there are echoes of 'atone for' and 'expiate'.[43] In Jesus' death on the cross we have 'a full expression of his love, and a full satisfaction of God's justice'.[44]

We can add further statements to this: Jesus came to show us the full expression of the kingdom, the full wholeness of transformation and restoration that God intends. The recovery of our ability to perceive the world and His kingdom as God intends is part of that fullness and should be understood within that fullness.

David Aune identifies different forms of prophecy embedded in the New Testament that we could miss. One of these he calls 'oracles of assurance'.[45] He also points out that oracles of assurance can include 'announcement of salvation'.[46]

---

[41] France, *The Gospel of Mark*, 420.

[42] France, *The Gospel of Mark*, 420.

[43] Edwards, *The Gospel According to Mark*, 327.

[44] Edwards, *The Gospel According to Mark*, 328.

[45] Aune, *Prophecy in Early Christianity and the Ancient Mediterranean World*, 321.

[46] Aune, *Prophecy in Early Christianity and the Ancient Mediterranean World*, 322.

An example of an oracle of assurance is Acts 18:9-10: 'One night the Lord spoke to Paul in a vision: "Do not be afraid; keep on speaking, do not be silent. For I am with you…"'

We can see that many of the things Jesus spoke to people are oracles of assurance and salvation. For example, when blind Bartimaeus is healed we read in Mark 10:51-52:

> 'What do you want me to do for you?' Jesus asked him.
> The blind man said, 'Rabbi, I want to see.'
> 'Go,' said Jesus, 'your faith has healed you.' Immediately he received his sight and followed Jesus along the road.

Bartimaeus here is probably asking not just for physical sight, but also for his spiritual eyes to be opened. That both happen can be seen not only in his physical healing, but also in his decision to follow Jesus along the 'way', symbolising discipleship and not just a physical road. Jesus' words, 'your faith has healed you', are words of both assurance and salvation.

I know that at one point in my own life someone spoke an oracle of salvation. That is how I heard it, and I believed in that moment. I can't remember the exact words but I do remember the physical, emotional and spiritual impact of them. The words had the power of an oracle for my life in that moment.

We cannot convert anyone, but we can witness, and through listening to God we can speak out the oracles of salvation and assurance that He intends for those we meet.

The Lord's Supper

There is another significant passage about Jesus as Saviour, and that occurs at the Lord's Supper in Mark 14:12-25. In particular, the key verses are 22-24:

> While they were eating, Jesus took bread, and when he had given thanks, he broke it and gave it to his disciples, saying, 'Take it; this is my body.'
>
> Then he took a cup, and when he had given thanks, he gave it to them, and they all drank from it.
>
> 'This is my blood of the covenant, which is poured out for many,' he said to them.

France summarises these verses: 'the bread represents Jesus' body and the wine his blood, and their reception of these elements symbolizes the beneficial effects of his imminent death.'[47] Again, what Mark writes is simple and yet profound. The symbolism is not exhausted, but echoes Jesus' previous words in Mark 10:45.

This is a Passover meal which is a remembrance of 'the rescue of God's covenant people from slavery and the lamb whose death was a necessary part of that deliverance'.[48] The theme of moving out of slavery into a new freedom of life in all its fullness is implicitly underlined through more Old Testament echoes from the Greek Septuagint version. Rikki E. Watts has written a whole thesis on how Isaiah's theme of the new exodus occurs in Mark's gospel.[49] The salvation Jesus offers can be conceptualised as a new exodus, a movement from slavery into freedom.

---

[47] France, *The Gospel of Mark*, 563.

[48] France, *The Gospel of Mark*, 563.

[49] Rikki E. Watts, *Isaiah's New Exodus in Mark* (Grand Rapids, Michigan: Baker Academic, 1997).

Mark outlines yet another way in which this happens. His gospel has a whole strand on demonic powers and Satan. His deep theology of these powers is that Satan has blinded those in the world and has them in bondage. Jesus has come as 'the stronger one' to break this bondage and restore people's sight (see Mark 3:27).[50]

Everything I have said so far about Jesus as Saviour who enables us to reperceive the world means He is engaging with our attentional capacities and transforming them. But the kingdom also demands our attentional capacities to be sharpened, restored and transformed, because of the mysterious, hidden nature of the kingdom. In the next chapter we will look at our attentional capacities for those reasons.

All the other aspects of Jesus' life that we are going to look at – Jesus as Seer, Sage, Storyteller and so on – can all be seen, not as discrete functions but as part of the kingdom that Jesus brings to us. As part of that kingdom, our *intention* can be focused on being with Him. We are working on our *attention* to develop a perceptive faith, and our *attitude*, like that of Jesus, needs to be one of serving and giving.

My experience of God's kingdom as 'creation healed' includes my own life. I am saving up to buy a piece of Japanese pottery called *Kintsukuroi* (golden repair), where a broken pot is intentionally and lovingly remade with gold and silver lacquer.

Back in 2006 I felt like I was falling apart. I was stressed, anxious, depressed and close to burnout. God repaired me with the gold and silver of His kingdom. One of the key points of being put back together was that He began to open my spiritual eyes. He helped me focus on things I'd been avoiding, things that were smaller than I'd imagined, and He

---

50 Joel Marcus, *Mark 8-16: Anchor Bible* (New York: Doubleday, 2009), 609.

helped me see that life could be so much more expansive than I had imagined – much more like the plains of my childhood than the narrow lanes of England. I saw through His eyes that I was worth repairing, and that I could be repaired. He opened windows on gifts He had given me that I hadn't yet found or believed in for myself. I now believe that His divine 'golden repair' of the kingdom is accessible to all.

Reflection

Intention

How might you find ways every day to be with Jesus?

Attention

Where have you been encouraged by other people modelling perceptive faith that you can learn from?

Attitude

Review your walk with Jesus now: where are you serving and giving, and with what attitude?

Chapter three
The attentional capacities we use

Read Mark 4, the kingdom parables.

Is mindfulness God given?

The cognitive neuroscience of attention and awareness uses the word 'mindfulness' as a generic word for our attentional capacities. Mindfulness as our universal, God-given human capacity for awareness and attention is part of natural and incarnational theology. Alister McGrath defines natural theology as an 'open secret' – that is, 'a publicly accessible entity, whose true meaning is known only from the standpoint of Christian faith'.[51] In that sense we look at nature from the standpoint of faith and discern its status as creation.

Jesus spoke about the kingdom as a secret *(mysterion)* which 'denotes not incomprehensibility but hiddenness'.[52] I will come to this when we talk about Jesus as Storyteller, but the nature of the hidden kingdom demands that we turn to our capacity for attention and awareness.

Mindfulness is a natural capacity, but it has Christian significance because it is a capacity that has been created by the Christian Creator God. In its created capacity it enables us

---

[51] McGrath, *The Open Secret,*16.

[52] France, *The Gospel of Mark,* 196.

to be aware and attentive to God, to others, to our own salvation, to creation and so on. This would not be the focus in secular psychology. Ironically, it is also an open secret in the sense that the world is open to it as a natural capacity, but it still seems to be a secret in much of the church. Indeed, it is feared by some in the church.

Defining mindfulness: it is part of being human

If we define mindfulness clearly, the fears some Christians have about it can be allayed. It is not simply a Buddhist construct, as some imagine and fear. It is part of being human. Because mindfulness is a universal (God-given) human capacity of attention and awareness, all the faith traditions work with it in some way, with different intentions and practices. However, it is the cognitive neuroscience of attention and awareness that can help us see mindfulness clearly as it is.

If you hold it up to the light of this empirical research, much as you might hold up a diamond, a complex, multi-faceted human capacity emerges. It is a capacity that can lead us to a beautiful mind.

Principally, mindfulness is awareness – our universal human capacity for awareness and attention.[53] Attention and awareness are central to human consciousness and perception, and so mindfulness can be defined as a quality of consciousness.

Because it is a quality of our consciousness, it has also been observed as a state of mind, and a trait or disposition that

---

[53] J. Mark G. Williams and Jon Kabat-Zinn, 'Mindfulness: Diverse Perspectives on its Meaning, Origins, and Multiple Applications at the Intersection of Science and Dharma', in *Mindfulness: Diverse Perspectives on its Meaning, Origins, and Applications*, eds. J. Mark G. Williams and Jon Kabat-Zinn (London: Routledge, 2013), 15.

occurs naturally within us as human beings. I want to focus particularly on this aspect of mindfulness, as a state and trait, which is often missed, although I do need to point out the other aspects of mindfulness too. As a trait it can be measured, and there are a number of scales that do this.[54]

Attention and awareness can also be broken down into key psychological processes such as the ability to focus attention, to sustain attention and to switch attention back to the object of focus when our mind wanders, as well as the ability to be openly aware of our internal and external environment. These processes enable us to regulate our emotions, to shift our cognitive perspective, and to respond wisely to stress rather than react automatically in unhelpful ways.

Research coming out of neuroscience supports this idea of mindfulness as a state of mind, a trait, with evidence about what they call neural correlates, the link between a process and a particular area of the brain connected to that process. In particular, neuroscientists have observed links with areas of the prefrontal cortex that are to do with emotional regulation.[55]

Mindfulness and meditation

All of this needs to be distinguished from the mindful awareness or meditative practices that enable us to become more mindful. The negative reaction to mindfulness for some Christians is also in part a reaction to the word 'meditation'.

---

[54] See Mark A. Lau et al, 'The Toronto Mindfulness Scale: Development and Validation', *Journal of Clinical Psychology* 62 no. 12 (2006), 1445-1467. Available at http://dx.doi.org/10.1002/jclp.20326.
[55] Richard Chambers, Eleonora Gullone and Nicholas B. Allen, 'Mindful Emotion Regulation: An Integrative Review', *Clinical Psychology Review* 29 (2009), 566. Available at http://dx.doi.org/10.1016/j.cpr.2009.06.005 (accessed 17th November 2015).

The word is often used without any clear understanding, and with no appreciation that there are different families of meditation. For example, mindfulness as embodied awareness and attention, which is about facing reality, is not the same as transcendental meditation. Within mindfulness, the word 'meditation' is simply to do with 'attentional training'.[56] Christian discipleship also has to do with attentional training: 'Do not *attend* to your own interests but rather to the interests of others.'[57]

Mindfulness as a trait or state of mind is not dependent on meditation. In fact, aerobic exercise can increase dispositional mindfulness,[58] as can simply cultivating our natural ability to notice things.

The other main strand of mindfulness is the therapies that are based on mindfulness or that incorporate it, such as Mindfulness-Based Stress Reduction (MBSR), and Mindfulness-Based Cognitive Therapy (MBCT). These have mainly been developed for mental health and psychological well-being, with MBSR having a number of applications, including stress, and MBCT particularly developed to help those with recurrent depression. They also incorporate sophisticated maps of how the mind-body works.

---

[56] Chambers et al., 'Mindful Emotion Regulation', 561.

[57] Philippians 2:4 as translated by Stephen E. Fowl in *Philippians: The Two Horizons New Testament Commentary* (Grand Rapids, Michigan: William B. Eerdmans Publishing Company, 2005), 77.

[58] Hendrik Mothes et al., 'Regular Aerobic Exercise Increases Dispositional Mindfulness in Men: A Randomized Controlled Trial', *Mental Health and Physical Activity* 7, no.2 (2014), 111.-119. Available at http://dx.doi.org/10.1016/j.mhpa.2014.02.003 (accessed 17th November 2015).

Christian distinctives

None of the above takes into account Christian distinctives of mindfulness, such as mindfulness of God, or ethical and relational aspects we would value that see this natural capacity as having a created element and purpose from God.

A thoughtless dismissal of mindfulness not only loses the richness of its created possibilities but also means that we are turning our back on a number of human abilities we could benefit from.

For example, let us take the central position of the sermon in our services. We hope that the congregation, through listening to the Word and the words, are *focusing their attention* on the passage and on what is being said. Sermons vary in length, but congregations can learn to listen for up to 40 minutes or more, in an act of *sustained attention*. If their minds wander, hopefully they have learnt to *switch their attention* back to the message. In this process we have the possibility of being *openly aware* to what God might be saying – a closed mind is of no help to bring change and transformation. During the message the congregation might be challenged about *regulating their emotion* through Paul's words to the Ephesians: 'do not let the sun go down while you are still angry' (4:26).

If we turn away from mindfulness, we turn our back on these processes of focused attention, sustained attention, emotional regulation and so on.

But there are other problems in not paying attention to what mindfulness teaches us and what is affirmed about attention and awareness within the biblical and historical tradition of the church.

We are often led out of our awareness by a self-focused attention that centres on anxious preoccupation with self and rumination, to the detriment of our mental health.[59] Jesus warns against this self-focused anxious and fearful attention when He says in Mark 8:35, 'For whoever wants to save their life will lose it.'

Traditionally, the church has been about developing deep attention: attentiveness to our need for transformation, to God, to the needs of others, to our stewardship of creation. Culturally, because of the virtual world we now live in, we are moving away from cultivating deep attention to what N. Katherine Hayles calls hyper attention, which 'has a low threshold for boredom, alternates flexibly between different information streams, and prefers a high level of stimulation'.[60] Because of this we are simply unable to focus on just one thing for any length of time. We are also much more likely to live our lives on autopilot, mindlessly and automatically reacting to people and events unwisely and without emotional regulation, usually in a narcissistic and self-centred way.

To come back to the standpoint of Christian faith with which I began, this discerning standpoint also enables us to shift our perspective. When a crisis happens in our life, and we are bounced by circumstances into a place of fear and doubt, our faith in God's care for us enables us to shift our perspective back to one of trust. That faith perspective relativises our human reactions and enables us to respond with trust.

The heart of Christian mindfulness lies in Jesus' statement to Peter in Mark 8:33: 'Get behind me, Satan! ... You do not have in mind the concerns of God, but merely human concerns.' By developing our capacity to be attentive and

---

[59] Mark A. Lau et al, 'The Toronto Mindfulness Scale: Development and Validation,', 1447.

[60] N. Katherine Hayles, *How We Think: Digital Media and Contemporary Technogenesis* (Chicago: The University of Chicago Press, 2012), 12.

aware in the present moment of ethical choice, we can mindfully choose the things of God over the human things jostling for our attention. But as we will discover, we are able, when we turn towards Jesus and enter His kingdom, to reperceive the world and the kingdom hidden within it. We are able to develop our prophetic insights – and also to live serving and giving in the way that Jesus modelled for us. *We can then develop a prophetic state of mind, which we will expand on later*. Our *intention* here, therefore, would be to develop this prophetic state of mind. We do this through daily spiritual practices.

Awareness is like gravity

Awareness (mindfulness) is like gravity in that it is a central part of our life, but we usually don't pay attention to it. Mindfulness as a practice enables us to walk freely within the gravitational pull (often negative, selfish and distorted) of our own minds.

Because mindfulness (awareness) is plastic, like our minds, it can be worked with in different ways. All the faith traditions discovered the gravity of awareness and attention early on, and work with it in different ways. It is in more recent times that Western science has started paying attention to it through research and the development of mindfulness-based and mindfulness-incorporating therapies.

Mindfulness for health

So what does mindfulness offer the Christian?

Christians are frail human beings, just like everyone else, and are as susceptible to psychological vulnerability as the next person – we live in the same stressful world. There are two main dimensions to mindfulness: mindfulness for health and mindfulness of God. Both should engage Christians.

In terms of mindfulness for health, the UK Mental Health Foundation's 2010 *Mindfulness Report* lists a number of significant mental health conditions for which mindfulness is being used, through a number of different mindfulness-based or mindfulness-incorporating therapies. These include depression, insomnia, anxiety disorders, stress, chronic pain, psoriasis, fibromyalgia, chronic fatigue syndrome, drug abuse, psychosis, eating disorders, self-harm, borderline personality disorder, as well as to improve mood and reduce stress for those being treated for cancer.[61] Many more conditions could be added.

When I look at this list, I don't just see medical terms; I see people. People I know and people who have had their distress alleviated through mindfulness therapies. This is why it matters for Christians, not just for Christians we know who are suffering from mental health conditions, but also because we should be concerned for the common good of all.

The main definition that secular psychology uses to define mindfulness, which I have mentioned before, is, 'Mindfulness means paying attention in a particular way: on purpose, in the present moment, and nonjudgmentally.'[62] Working in this way enables a shift in perspective, where we don't try to change our afflictive thoughts and feelings; we change our relationship to them. Thoughts therefore are seen just as passing mental events and people 'no longer relate *from* their

---

[61] Mental Health Foundation (2010), *Mindfulness Report*, London, 9-10.

[62] Kabat-Zinn, *Wherever You Go, There You Are*, quoted in Segal, Williams and Teasdale, *Mindfulness-Based Cognitive Therapy for Depression*, 40.

thoughts but *to* their thoughts, as objects of awareness.'[63] In this way we move from being a victim of our thoughts to being a witness to them.

Mindfulness of God

In this book I am looking at the other side of the coin – less at mindfulness for health and much more at the benefits that mindfulness of God brings. This is a neglected aspect.

I first came across mindfulness in secular psychology when I was studying counselling at Roehampton University part-time, and suffering myself from stress, anxiety and depression. Very close to burnout, I started using mindful awareness practices and found them very helpful. At the same time, a little book called *The Jesus Prayer* by former Bishop of Coventry, Simon Barrington-Ward, almost jumped off the bookshelf at me. This ancient Christian mindful awareness practice, 'Lord Jesus Christ Son of God, have mercy on me a sinner,' is used repetitively with the breath in an embodied way. When I started using it, it helped to ease my anxiety.

I realised that there was a lot of overlap between what secular mindfulness was saying in terms of working with afflictive thoughts and what the early Christian contemplatives were saying.

When it comes to mindfulness of God, I am reminded of Genesis 26:15: 'So all the wells that his father's servants had dug in the time of his father Abraham, the Philistines stopped up, filling them with earth.' Mindfulness is one of our ancient spiritual wells, but it is not anyone else who has filled it in; we have done that ourselves by ignoring the biblical witness to awareness and attention, and the Christian contemplative tradition which is concerned with mindfulness of God.

---

[63] Segal et al., *Mindfulness-Based Cognitive Therapy for Depression*, 248.

As I began to research the Jesus Prayer as a form of watchfulness (another form of mindfulness for Christians), I came across this phrase from fifth-century Greek Bishop Diadochus of Photike, a pioneer of the Jesus Prayer: 'Let us keep our eyes always fixed on the depths of our heart with an unceasing *mindfulness* of God.'[64] In *A Time to Heal*, a report for the Anglican House of Bishops on the ministry of healing, the authors make the point, 'Jesus' healing ministry was also one of the restoration of vision. Jesus came into the world and it was a place of darkness, a place of a lack of the vision of God.'[65] Mindfulness of God enables us to restore our broken, fragmented and distorted vision of God, and frees us to see with His eyes rather than our own. In this sense, mindfulness of God is central to our discipleship goal of becoming like Christ.

In addition to using secular mindful awareness practices for health and to turn down the noise in our heads (also good for our prayer lives), we can use ancient Christian meditative practices like *Lectio Divina*, a slow meditative reading of Scripture inherited from the Jewish tradition, and the Jesus Prayer which also helps us to still our minds and be watchful and mindful of God. Above all, we cultivate what Jesus commends and the early church called *diorasis*, a clear seeing, discernment or spiritual insight.

David Aune says in his book on prophecy in early Christianity that oracles of judgement, though common in the Old Testament, are 'exceedingly rare in early Christianity'.[66]

---

[64] My italics. Quoted in Olivier Clement, *The Roots of Christian Mysticism* (London: New City, 2002), 204.

[65] *A Time to Heal – A Report for the House of Bishops on the Healing Ministry* (Church House Publishing, 2007), 20.

[66] Aune, *Prophecy in Early Christianity and the Ancient Mediterranean World*, 323.

Jesus Himself passes judgement on the Temple (Mark 13:2), but we need to ensure that in our own practice we mirror the early church in the rarity of our announcements of judgement.

I think the idea of *diorasis*, a clear seeing, is what is needed. When the truth is presented in love and compassion and is received as 'bringing us into the light', then we can receive the truth. We live in a very critical and judgemental culture, which seeks to shame people. Our approach should be very different.

Mindfulness as a human capacity is a collection of jigsaw pieces. The interesting thing is that with these pieces we can make different jigsaw puzzles. The central strand of these puzzles is to do with healing, wholeness and the transformation of our perceptive faculties. Mindfulness matters for Christians, not just for ourselves, but also for our neighbours, for God, and for creation itself. We need to learn and have a map of what our *attentional capacities* are, and our *attitude* should be one of openness, gratitude and curiosity in exploring these capacities.

I would also urge you to use the Ananias Prayer to help develop this clear compassionate seeing that I have commended. You can read more about it in *A Book of Sparks*,[67] but here it is below. We pray first for ourselves, then for friends and family, then for a stranger, and then for an enemy. Finally we pray it for ourselves again.

> May the love of Christ take hold of me;
> May the light of Christ shine in my heart;
> May the love of Christ flow through me like a river.

and then:

---

[67] Shaun Lambert, *A Book of Sparks: A Study in Christian MindFullness*, second edition (Watford: Instant Apostle, 2014), 134.

May the love of Christ take hold of him/her;
May the light of Christ shine in his/her heart;
May the love of Christ flow through him/her like a
river.

Reflection

Intention

Try to cultivate a state of mind where you are quiet, still and able to be fully open to God's promptings.

Attention

Review what this chapter says about attention and awareness.

Attitude

In order to develop an open, curious attitude into attention and awareness, do some research on mindfulness, attention and awareness, or try to notice how many times you come across references to it in the media.

Chapter four
Jesus and the senses – the embodied gospel

Read the first five chapters of Mark's gospel and try to notice any references to the senses or the involvement of the body in what is written. Alternatively, listen to an audio recording of the gospel and let your ears be your attentive antennae.

The embodied gospel

Recent scholarship recognises that the gospel as presented by Jesus (and it is quite clear in all four gospels) is an embodied gospel. If I were to say to you, 'What do baptism, the Lord's Supper (Communion), the kiss of peace and table fellowship all have in common?' The answer should be that *they all involve the body!*

For too long the church has lived by a Gnostic heresy that the spirit is good and the body is bad. We need to reclaim what both the Old and New Testaments say about the body. The Bible is not dualistic about body and spirit, but recognises that our different human capacities are integrated into a whole that is embodied, relational and communitarian, and focused on God.

This is often where we have read our Western preconceptions into Scripture. Why is this important? I hear so many Christians who want to experience what Jesus promised we would experience, yet they say, 'I never hear God speak to me!' Or, 'Other people talk about experiencing the Holy Spirit in their life but I never experience anything.' Other people tell me they never receive any prophetic insights.

I believe the central problem lies not with those committed Christians but in how they have been taught to ignore their embodied senses and capacity for attention and awareness, whether that is implicitly (usually the case) or explicitly.

As the church we have taken on the clothes of Western culture which focuses very much on rational, critical thinking, of living in our heads and ignoring our bodies and our embodied awareness.

Accessing the transcendent

To repeat what I quoted from Alister McGrath in the introduction, 'It is merely to assert that for human beings in this world the transcendent is accessed and the spiritual life is expressed exclusively through the medium of our material bodies.'[68]

God will speak to us through all the senses He has given us. How may senses do we have? Traditionally we believe we have five senses. Daniel Siegel, an interpersonal neurobiologist, says we have eight.

What Daniel Siegel says is based on empirical research and is science fact, not science fiction, and we could even add other senses. The sixth sense is that we can be aware of what is going on in our bodies; the seventh sense is that we can be aware of some of what we are thinking and feeling; and the eight sense is a relational sense – we can pick up other people's thoughts and feelings because they leak. This eighth

---

[68] McGrath, *The Open Secret*, 82.

sense is why we are able to have counsellors and ministers and spiritual directors, and empathic listening.[69]

I would add a ninth sense, which is the ability to become aware of the presence of God. But when we come into the presence of our Creator all our senses resonate with that experience – and this is what we would call awe, wonder and reverence – a true fear of God, not the fear we experience when we see a snake, for example. So our *intention* here must be to practise coming to our senses as often as possible. We need to learn to inhabit our bodies again. In our resonant bodies we inhabit the world of perception, not just the world of rational, critical thinking which is where we are culturally stuck, and where the church has also often got stuck. Our senses are simply streams of awareness within us, which God has created.

But is not just the embodied gospel that has been neglected, and it is not just that attention and awareness in the Bible has been neglected; we have also neglected to explore the many times that the senses appear in Scripture. This is now being addressed in scholarship.

Louise Lawrence has engaged with sensory anthropology and disability in a recent book on the gospels.[70] We have often skipped references to the senses when reading the Bible from a Western perspective, because we have over-valued rational, critical thinking. My sense is that embodied awareness and attention and the senses were much more important in the Ancient Near East and the gospels than we have given them credit for.

---

[69] Daniel J. Siegel, *The Mindful Brain* (New York: W.W. Norton & Company, 2007), 122-3.

[70] Louise, J. Lawrence, *Sense and Stigma in the Gospels: Depictions of Sensory-Disabled Characters* (Oxford: Oxford University Press, 2013).

Lawrence has analysed Mark's gospel for what she calls a 'sense-scape'.[71] I would say this is part of a whole landscape of consciousness and language of perception in Mark's gospel.

The power of Jesus' words and actions

One of Lawrence's most important observations is the nature of Jesus' speech as prophetic and inspired, but in a particular way. She states, 'Jesus beckons people to follow him primarily through speech commands (1:17).'[72]

She adds, 'For Mark words have not only dramatic but also bodily force.'[73] This applies to Jesus in any of His interrelated capacities as Saviour, Seer, Sage or Storyteller. It also means that we can broadly define prophetic insight that is spoken out as a speech-act; we should know that it has power. It is not, as in many charismatic subcultures, about blessings of health, wealth and prosperity in the future; it is something that transforms our direction and life.

These speech-acts are also called transformative language.[74] Alexandra Brown, in describing transformative language, is looking at 1 Corinthians and Paul's preaching about the cross. She writes, 'Paul's aim in preaching the cross is to alter his hearer's perception of the world in such a way as to alter their experience *in* the world.'[75] Mark's gospel has been described as an extended narrative about Jesus' suffering (passion) and the cross. All the way through Mark's gospel, what we read or hear about Jesus' life and ministry does exactly the same thing

---

[71] Lawrence, *Sense and Stigma in the Gospels*, 14.

[72] Louise Lawrence, 'Exploring the Sense-scape of the Gospel of Mark', *Journal for the Study of the New Testament* 33, no.4 (2011), 391.

[73] Lawrence, Exploring the Sense-scape of the Gospel of Mark', 391.

[74] Alexandra R. Brown, *The Cross and Human Transformation* (Minneapolis: Fortress Press, 1995), xviii.

[75] Brown, *The Cross and Human Transformation*, xviii.

– Mark is seeking to alter his hearer's perception *of* the world in such a way as to alter their experience *in* the world.

I received my call into the ministry 21 years ago in a crisis experience in a cattle shed at New Wine's annual conference in Shepton Mallet. I felt God saying, 'Take up the word of God which is the sword of the Spirit.' At the same time I saw a picture of a hand holding up a sword or cross of light. It was an embodied experience with the force of prophetic language, in that I knew in my heart, bones and blood that God was calling me, and in the moment I was transformed enough to seek to follow that calling into ministry. It was prophetic speech that acted on me, that had power to change me.

As I say, we will come back to this central definition of prophetic speech.

What else can we say about the senses and the embodied nature of Mark's gospel? In Mark 1 Jesus goes to the *home* of Simon and Andrew – there is no sacred/secular divide with Him. The kingdom is at our work and in our homes. We may see them as private; Jesus sees them as abodes of the kingdom.

Simon's mother-in-law was in bed with a fever, and we are told in verse 31 that Jesus 'went to her, took her hand and helped her up. The fever left her and she began to wait on them.' When Jesus *touches* her, she is healed. Touch as a sense features ten times in Mark's gospel.[76]

This is another aspect of Jesus as Saviour and healer: He is filled with the contagious holiness of God. He breaks the social codes of the day in touching women, dead bodies and lepers. We see that almost immediately after He has healed Simon's mother-in-law, He touches and heals a leper, which would make Him ritually unclean (1:41). This gives us another key insight into what it means to be a prophet. *A prophet's attention is free from the gravitational pull of the culture within which they*

---

[76] Lawrence, 2011, 390.

live. Each culture captures our attention in different ways; we need to learn to set it free. N. Katherine Hayles says the limited resource in our culture is attention: 'There is too much to attend to and too little time to do it.'[77] Bernard Stiegler would go further than this, and Hayles summarises his position as 'attention is actively being *destroyed* by what he calls the audiovisual (i.e. film and television) and programming industries'.[78] Stiegler's own vivid phrase is that we are the victims of 'psychotechnical attention capture'.[79]

That we are psychologically captured in terms of our attention (which directs the focus and path of our life) is borne out by all the research into the virtual world in which we live, which includes the loss of deep attention and the rise of the hyper attention I have mentioned already.

Jesus and embodied awareness

Instead of limiting our view on the world to the traditional Western five senses, we should consider the possibility of more. As we consider this, we can see another sense at work in Mark 2.

At the beginning of Mark 2 we read that Jesus has 'come home', and the people of Capernaum crowd into and around the home. Four men 'unroof' the house and lower down a paralysed man for Jesus to heal.

When Jesus says in verse 5, 'Son, your sins are forgiven,' some of the teachers of the law think in their hearts (not out loud, or in a way someone could physically hear), 'Why does

---

[77] Hayles, *How We Think*, 12.

[78] Bernard Stiegler, *Taking Care of Youth and the Generations* (Stanford, California: Stanford University Press, 2010), summarized by Hayles, *How We Think*, 251.

[79] Bernard Stiegler, *Taking Care of Youth and the Generations*, 58, quoted by Hayles, *How We Think*, 251.

this fellow talk like that? He's blaspheming! Who can forgive sins but God alone?'(2:7).

The next verse tells us, 'Immediately Jesus knew in his spirit that this was what they were thinking in their hearts.'

Here we have Daniel Siegel's eighth relational sense at work. It is a natural capacity enhanced by the Holy Spirit – one we can cultivate too: the ability to pick up other people's thoughts and feelings. But in the ethical moment of choice, Jesus is free to do the right thing, the prophetic thing, regardless of the pressure to conform to the religious leaders or other cultural assumptions.

In Mark 5 we have the story of Jesus raising a 12-year-old girl from the dead, sandwiching the story of the woman who has been subject to bleeding for 12 years (5:25). This woman approaches Jesus secretly as He is surrounded by a crowd, in order to touch His cloak. Her reasoning (prophetic insight) is that, 'If I just touch his clothes, I will be healed' (5:28).

In a beautiful piece of detail which we often miss, and which highlights our embodied senses, we read in verse 29, after she has touched Him, 'Immediately her bleeding stopped and she *felt in her body* that she was freed from her suffering' (italics added). This is the sixth embodied sense at work: knowing what is going on in our bodies. The next verse says, 'At once Jesus realised that power had gone out from him.' Again, this is the sixth embodied sense being referenced. It is also an example of how Daniel Siegel defines presence – receptive awareness to whatever arises in the moment.

In Siegel's book, *The Mindful Brain*, the author talks about the mindful awareness induced by poetry, creating what he calls 'a receptive presence of mind'.[80] About 'presence' he says,

---

[80] Siegel, *The Mindful Brain*, 161.

'I mean quite specifically the state of receptive awareness of our open minds to whatever arises as it arises.'[81]

A prophet has that receptive awareness. It can be cultivated and developed and inhabited. This uses the word 'presence' in a slightly different sense to the idea in Mark's gospel of Jesus being present to His disciples (he called them to 'be with him' – 3:14). Here, relational presence is transformative and life-changing. But Jesus was also full of receptive awareness to what was going on around Him in the present moment, in hidden dimensions as well.

A moment of prophetic insight happens when God takes our God-given capacity for open receptive awareness and overlays it with revelation from the Holy Spirit. Jesus underlines this near the end of Mark, in 13:11: 'Whenever you are arrested and brought to trial, do not worry beforehand about what to say. Just say whatever is given you at the time, for it is not you speaking, but the Holy Spirit.'

In Mark, as I've mentioned, some words, themes and concepts don't occur very often, and that is what makes them important. The Holy Spirit is one such example. We begin with a reference to the Holy Spirit as John prophesies about Jesus (Mark 1:8): 'I baptise you with water, but he will baptise you with the Holy Spirit.' Everything Jesus does to transform people is through immersion in the Holy Spirit, as this verse promises.

1 Corinthians 6:19 brings together the body and the Holy Spirit: 'Do you not know that your bodies are temples of the Holy Spirit, who is in you, whom you have received from God?' Many of the difficult emotions we face – shame, guilt, anxiety, anger – are embodied emotions. Because we try to regulate these emotions by avoiding them, we end up not living in our bodies. Paradoxically, the Holy Spirit can help us

---

[81] Siegel, *The Mindful Brain*, 161.

receive back our bodies, because the idea of the body as a 'temple' tells us that it is not bad. In fact, our bodies are very honest and tell us the truth of what is going on internally. This means that signals from the body can be signs from God that carry prophetic significance. Just as soils of the earth can take on a different colour because of something else within them, so our bodies can carry the colour and influence of the Holy Spirit.

Reflection

Intention

Our intention in this chapter is to work on developing a prophetic state of mind.

Attention

Pay attention to your words: are they healing or wounding? How much is your attention captured by the virtual world in which you live?

Attitude

Are you dismissive of this whole focus on working on our attention and awareness?

Chapter five
Jesus as Seer

Read Mark 8:31-33; 9:30-32; 10:32-34.

Jesus and his Jewish background

Jesus as Seer is standing within His Jewish heritage, and yet He makes His identity as a prophet unique through what He says and does.

Jesus refers to Himself as a prophet, and He is referred to publicly as a prophet (Mark 6:4; 6:14-15; 8:28). Ben Witherington III makes the point that Jesus is not a court prophet (like Nathan).[82] He does bear similarities to the northern prophets like Elijah and Elisha who do miracles; indeed, Mark makes such a point in Jesus 'passing by' (literal translation and echo of the Septuagint translation of the Elijah and Elisha story in 1 Kings 19:19-20) Simon and Andrew before calling them to follow Him (1:16), just as Elijah passed by Elisha.[83] When He is in Jerusalem He then speaks oracles, as did the southern prophets.[84]

One of the other interesting things, when we look at the landscape of prophecy in the Ancient Near East, is that

---

[82] Ben Witherington III, *Jesus the Seer: The Progress of Prophecy* (Minneapolis: Fortress Press, (2014), 248.

[83] Witherington, *Jesus the Seer*, 251,

[84] Witherington, *Jesus the Seer*, 251.

prophecy and prophets were widespread. This was a polytheistic world (outside of the Hebrew monotheistic worldview), and a prophet would speak on behalf of a god, claiming divine revelation.[85]

This meant, of course, that within the Old Testament or Hebrew Scriptures (but also true within the New Testament), one had to learn to distinguish between true prophets and false prophets (Isaiah 44:25; Matthew 7:15). But the fact that prophecy was so widespread suggests, I believe, that a natural capacity was being used in the process. The question then is, 'Who or what is providing the revelation?'

We also know that there were prophetesses in the Old and New Testaments (Judges 4:4; Acts 21:9). There are three main words used for a prophet in the Old Testament: an early word *Hozeh* or 'seer', which is used of Samuel, as is the more common word *nabi*.[86] The other word for seer sometime seen is *ro-eh*.[87]

What can we say about Jesus as Seer in Mark? To summarise what we have said so far, we need to remember that what is said about Jesus as Seer has to be held in the context of Him as Saviour, Sage, Storyteller and transformer of our embodied senses. When we put on Jesus as the 'Wakeful One', we ourselves are to be wakeful, alert and watchful for whatever God wants. If the prophet is concerned with the things of God, then God might ask him or her to be concerned with a great number of things that God is concerned about.

The character traits we are to develop are important as well. This is why I personally do not claim to be a prophet, but I

---

85 Witherington, *Jesus the Seer*, 2.

86 Witherington, *Jesus the Seer*, 20. See for example 1 Samuel 9:9 where two of the three main words appear.

87 Witherington, *Jesus the Seer*, 44. See also 2 Samuel 24:11, where two of the words appear in the same verse.

acknowledge that sometimes God has used me to bring prophetic insight. This is insight that I am not testifying about but that others have said to me, 'That spoke to me!' I believe one of the things to look for in someone operating in the prophetic is humility, and that they are not just after a title of 'prophet' because their ego needs a boost (Colossians 3:12). And so as we work on our *attitude*, humility is something that needs to be part of it.

Interestingly, another of the forms of prophecy that David Aune identifies as oracles concerns a call to a particular action, or behaviour, including 'ethical issues'.[88] He cites some examples, including 2 Thessalonians 3:6: 'In the name of the Lord Jesus Christ, we command you, brothers and sisters, to keep away from every believer who is idle and disruptive and does not live according to the teaching you received from us.' In Acts 13:2 we read, 'While they were worshipping the Lord and fasting, the Holy Spirit said, "Set apart for me Barnabas and Saul for the work to which I have called them."'[89]

In testing such prophetic words there needs to be discernment. There is a requirement for self-examination on the part of those receiving such words, as well as those giving them, especially if there is an ethical dimension involved.

There is also the need to choose the right moment. In the Greek there are a number of words that describe time. We know *chronos*, from which we get chronological time, but we don't always know the important of *kairos*, the right moment, the opportune moment. In fact, every moment is pregnant with the possibility of meeting God. This is what Jesus means

---

[88] Aune, *Prophecy in Early Christianity and the Ancient Mediterranean World*, 321. He calls this prescriptive or parenetic (concerning ethical issues).

[89] Aune, *Prophecy in Early Christianity and the Ancient Mediterranean World*, 321.

at the beginning of Mark's gospel in 1:15 when He says, 'The time has come ... The kingdom of God has come near.' The time here is *kairos* time.

Self-examination is a biblical theme that seems to have faded from our ethical awareness. In Mark's gospel, after Jesus prophesies at the Last Supper that one of the disciples would betray Him, we read in Mark 14:19, 'They were saddened, and one by one they said to him, "Surely you don't mean me?"'

There is here a *prophetic self-examination* in response to the impact of Jesus' prophetic words. This is another dimension that needs to be added to our disciple-making, especially as we seek to mature the prophetic insights that people have. One of the ways we can prophetically examine ourselves is through spiritual practices like *Lectio Divina* and the Jesus Prayer.

At the heart of Jesus' prophetic being is watchfulness. He commands this watchfulness for us, and it is a command which in the Greek is present continuous: we are to go on being watchful (Mark 13:37).

Jesus became watchful Himself through His disciplined habit of seeking silence and solitude in order to pray (Mark 1:35-39). Let's make that our *intention* as well.

As we look at the detail of Mark's gospel, another luminous pattern emerges.

Prophetic seeing

This is Mark's use of the word ἰδὼν ('seeing'), which the Markan Jesus does a number of times at critical junctures (1:16; 2:5, 14; 3:34; 5:6; 6:34, 48; 8:33; 9:25; 10:14, 21, 23, 27; 11:13; 12:34), giving it a greater meaning than just physical seeing.

If we take the first occasion in Mark 1:16, we can hear the voice of the gospel speaker and writer: 'As Jesus walked beside the Sea of Galilee, he saw Simon and his brother Andrew casting a net into the lake, for they were fishermen.'

As previously highlighted, the Greek word translated 'walked beside' is *paragon*, which literally means 'passing by'. Joel Marcus also sees this as an echo of Elijah passing by Elisha in 1 Kings 19:19 in that commissioning passage.[90]

What Marcus goes on to say is very significant. This seeing is 'an active, "possessive gaze" by means of which Jesus lays claim to something through a thorough inspection of it'.[91] This thorough inspection is a *clear, intense prophetic seeing* – He sees people, their potential, what they might do for the kingdom. Too often I think we have made prophetic insight impersonal and just about words given, whereas here you see the centrality of people in Jesus' prophetic gaze. His gaze is loving, compassionate, truthful, and full of light and insight.

This is another way we can broaden our understanding of who can be prophetic and in what way, without taking on the 'specialist' mantle of being a prophet. Pastors need to seek the prophetic insight that sees people as Jesus saw them, with the eyes of the kingdom, to help them find their place in the kingdom. We are looking for the charismature, not the charismaniac here. Too often I think people have become self-styled prophets because of self-focused attention rather than paying attention to others. As we saw earlier, Stephen Fowl translates Philippians 2:4, 'Do not *attend* to your own interests but rather to the interests of others.' We can work with our *attention* in this relational way in this chapter.

Our call to be prophetic, all of us, as a priesthood of all believers, is set within the context of the perceptive faith to which the Markan Jesus calls us. That is why Paul can say in 1 Corinthians 14:1, 'Follow the way of love and eagerly desire

---

[90] Joel Marcus, *Mark 1-8*, 179.

[91] Marcus, *Mark 1-8*, 183.

gifts of the Spirit, especially prophecy.' It is a perceptive faith that we are looking to cultivate.

Importantly, in our quest to find Jesus the Seer in Mark's gospel, as we have mentioned, we know that three times He prophesied His suffering, death and resurrection (8:31-33; 9:30-32; 10:32-34). We will come back to this and its significance, but for now let us pick up some other important aspects in the gospel.

Jesus is a teacher in Mark's gospel, one who has prophetic authority from the beginning, as in Mark 1:22: 'The people were *amazed* at his teaching, because he taught them as one who had *authority*, not as the teachers of the law' (italics added). Prophetic words are received and experienced as authoritative, which can be seen alongside what I have already said about them as speech-acts – they have a transformational impact on us.

Embodied and enacted prophetic actions

Mark's gospel is full of a family of words like *amazed* which describe people's full and embodied response to Jesus as Saviour, Seer, Sage, Storyteller and so on. Read the gospel again and try to track these words.

Jesus Himself carries out embodied and enacted prophetic actions. When He heals the blind man at Bethsaida (Mark 8:22-26), it is a two-stage healing. The man does not see clearly the first time. This healing is in a Markan sandwich with the healing of Bartimaeus in Mark 10:46-52 – in between we have the incomprehension of the disciples towards Jesus' death on a cross.

These physical healings are prophetically symbolic of the deeper spiritual restoration of sight that is required. Significantly, it is the cross that opens our spiritual eyes above all things. After Jesus' death on the cross we read, 'And when the centurion, who stood there in front of Jesus, saw how he died, he said, "Surely this man was the Son of God!"' (Mark 15:39). The centurion's spiritual eyes are opened at the foot of the cross.

In Mark 11, the theme of enacted and embodied prophetic actions continues. Jesus rides into Jerusalem on a colt (verses 1-10). This is a prophetic action in fulfilment of Old Testament prophecy about the messiah (Zechariah 9:9).

Jesus Himself recognises that He is a prophet. In His home town he says, 'A prophet is not without honour except in his own town' (Mark 6:4).

What I am trying to arrive at here is a picture of Jesus as a prophet, and the nature of the prophetic things He did. This gives us a picture of what prophetic insight might look like for us. For example, modelling prophetic service in a culture that is 'all about me' may well carry the force of a speech-act. The difference comes from any act of service because we are doing it with prophetic force, and the Holy Spirit gives it meaning to those looking on.

Prophets in the Old Testament were also asked to perform prophetic actions – for example, Jeremiah being asked to smash a clay jar to symbolise what would happen to Judah (Jeremiah 19).

There is a clear illustration elsewhere in Mark that this enacted prophecy can be part of the witness of an ordinary follower of Christ. In Mark 14 Jesus is anointed by a woman who does not say anything, but whose actions speak volumes. Jesus makes clear that the anointing is a prophetic enacted and embodied action: 'She poured perfume on my body beforehand to prepare for my burial' (14:8).

It is significant that this prophetic action is by a woman. What is powerful is that she recognises prophetically that Jesus must die on a cross – that He must suffer. When Jesus prophesies about His death and asks the male disciples to turn with Him and face it themselves, they refuse to do so and are guilty of experiential avoidance. They do not want to face the reality that the way of the cross is the way of suffering. Jesus Himself, in allowing her to anoint Him, and breaking all social boundaries, is also acting prophetically – particularly to place women on an equal footing in terms of discipleship and the prophetic. In Mark's gospel we see a very positive picture of women as disciples.

Remembering prophetically

Another thing that we learn from Mark's gospel is about remembering prophetically. Remembering is a key word that appears just three times in Mark's gospel, but each time it makes a very significant point.

The first time it appears, Jesus is talking to the disciples about the importance of having perceptive faith, and remembering prophetically something that has just happened (a kingdom miracle). In Mark 8 Jesus has just fed 4,000 people. The disciples show their lack of perception straight afterwards and Jesus says, 'Do you still not see or understand? Are your hearts hardened? Do you have eyes but fail to see, and ears but fail to hear? And don't you remember?' (8:17-18).

A disciple (who has prophetic insight) becomes a disciple through their spiritual eyes and ears being opened and their heart being softened, and by developing an ability to remember prophetically. The word 'remember' here in the Greek is *mnēmoneuete*, and is from an important family of words. These words also carry the meaning of being mindful, which in the context of Scripture is to remember in a particular way.

One of the things we are asked to do as disciples is to remember the things of God (Mark 8:33). Then in the moment of prophetic need we can remember prophetically – the thing of God comes to mind. All the great prophets immersed themselves in Scripture, and Jesus was no exception. If we also do that, Colossians 3:16 becomes a reality: 'Let the message of Christ dwell among you richly'. Then the Spirit of God can bring to mind with prophetic force something remembered out of our own inner library of Scripture.

There are two examples of this in Mark's gospel. Jesus underlines the importance of remembering prophetically in Mark 8:17-19, and this is followed up by Peter remembering two things prophetically. Jesus curses the fig tree in a prophetic action in 11:12-14 (the fig tree is symbolic of Israel). The next day Peter sees the fig tree withered and in verse 21 says, 'Peter *remembered* and said to Jesus, "Rabbi, Look! The fig-tree you cursed has withered!"' (italics added). The Greek word here is *anamnēstheis*, which is part of that family of words I have already mentioned.

In Mark 14 Jesus predicts that His disciples (including Peter) will all fall away. Peter denies this will happen but Jesus replies, 'Truly I tell you ... today – yes, tonight – before the cock crows twice you yourself will disown me three times' (14:30).

The cock does crow and it hits Peter with prophetic force:

> Immediately the cock crowed the second time. Then Peter remembered the word Jesus had spoken to him: 'Before the cock crows twice you will disown me three times.' And he broke down and wept.
> *Mark 14:72*

A prophetic state of mind

Jesus demonstrates a prophetic state of mind throughout the gospel.

When He is baptised (Mark 1:10-11), 'he saw heaven being torn open and the Spirit descending on him like a dove. And a voice came from heaven: "You are my Son, whom I love; with you I am well pleased."' This is significant as we begin the gospel, and there is no sense that the Spirit leaves Him at any point during His ministry (what happens on the cross would need to be examined elsewhere in Scripture).

He knew in His spirit what some teachers of the law were thinking in their hearts (2:8).

He 'sees' Simon and his brother Andrew and prophetically calls them to follow Him (1:16-17).

In Mark 2:14 He prophetically 'sees' Levi the tax collector and calls him to follow as well (and he does).

When He is questioned, He is able to give an answer in the moment that is full of prophetic insight (Mark 2:19).

There are many examples like this. You might want to reread chapter three on our attentional capacities, because the key question is, 'How do I develop this prophetic state of mind?' The answer is by developing our God-given capacity for attention and awareness – by developing deep attention and resisting the pressure of our virtual culture to fragment, and take captive that capacity.

Jesus models a life of attentive prayer for us in Mark 1:35: 'Very early in the morning, while it was still dark, Jesus got up, left the house and went off to a solitary place, where he prayed.'

Jesus finds solitude and silence and is focused in His attention. When the disciples tell Him that the crowds are looking for Him, He is not distracted but says, 'Let us go somewhere else…' (1:38).

It may be that fasting in the desert where He was tempted by Satan also played a part in developing His capacities for attention, awareness and prophetic insight (1:13). Again, it is the Spirit that sends Him out (1:12), and the prophet will always be a person of the Spirit: 'There are different kinds of gifts, but the same Spirit distributes them' (1 Corinthians 12:4).

Paul goes on to say that prophecy is one of those spiritual gifts (1 Corinthians 12:10).

This prophetic state of mind may be what the early church called *diorasis*, a clear seeing, discernment or spiritual insight, about which I will say more in chapter eight, on the Desert Sages and Seers. This state of mind is free from the gravitational pull of the culture within which a person lives. Let us also remember that prophetic insight may be picked up discerningly from any of our God-given senses, as we have already explained. Living too much in our heads, and separating the spiritual from the physical, may explain why many Christians feel they have not had spiritual experiences or prophetic insights.

This prophetic state of mind, I believe, is often experienced in preaching – and so we can widen our often narrow definitions of prophecy (and preaching). I prepare for preaching by reading the passage every day in a slow meditative way (*Lectio Divina*) weeks in advance. Only when it is richly dwelling inside me do I move to commentaries and other resources. I also preach without a script, and pray on a Sunday morning in such a way, through further meditative reading of Scripture and the use of contemplative prayers like the Jesus Prayer, that I might arrive at church in a prophetic state of mind – ready to listen to God in the moment of preaching, and respond to the movements of God's Holy Spirit. Prophecy cannot be reduced to preaching, but it plays an important part in preaching.

The prophetic state of mind will also play a part in what David Aune calls 'eschatological theophany oracles'.[92] I think Stephen's vision in Acts 7:55-56 could be seen in this way:

---

[92] Aune, *Prophecy in Early Christianity and the Ancient Mediterranean World*, 325.

> But Stephen, full of the Holy Spirit, looked up to heaven and saw the glory of God, and Jesus standing at the right hand of God. 'Look,' he said, 'I see heaven open and the Son of Man standing at the right hand of God.'

Here, the importance of the Holy Spirit is underlined in terms of bringing us to the state of mind where we can see 'heaven open' and the 'glory of God'.

Jesus as eschatological prophet

From Mark's gospel I have to mention Jesus as an eschatological prophet: He does speak about the end times and His return, particularly in chapter 13. There is also His clearing of the temple courts in Mark 11:15-17, which is an enacted prophetic action of judgement on the temple. This is followed by His prophecy at the beginning of chapter 13 about the destruction of the temple (13:1-2).

What I want to underline here is that Jesus makes it very clear that we are not to be looking to the future trying to set a date for His return: 'But about that day or hour no one knows, not even the angels in heaven, nor the Son, but only the Father' (13:32).

In fact, He tells us to be watching in the present moment for the signs of the end times:

> 'Now learn this lesson from the fig-tree: as soon as its twigs get tender and its leaves come out, you know that summer is near. Even so, when you see these things happening, you know that it is near, right at the door.'
> *Mark 13:28-29*

This watching in the present moment is underlined in His parable about this eschatological watching:

> 'Be on guard! Be alert! You do not know when that time will come. It's like a man going away: he leaves his house and puts his servants in charge, each with their assigned task, and tells the one at the door to keep watch.
>
> 'Therefore keep watch because you do not know when the owner of the house will come back – whether in the evening, or at midnight, or when the cock crows, or at dawn. If he comes suddenly, do not let him find you sleeping. What I say to you, I say to everyone: "Watch!"'
> *Mark 13:33-37*

This parable is saturated with the language of perception, applied to our eschatological watchfulness. In verse 33 we have two examples. The first is *agrypneite*, which is about being wakeful, and then *blepete*, which is about being alert and attentive. Variations of the verb *blepó* occur 15 times in Mark's gospel. The other key word is *grēgorē*, and variations thereof from the verb *grégoreó*, meaning 'to watch'. This occurs six times in Mark's gospel.

Some detailed examination of the primary text of Mark's gospel, beginning with the two key words he uses for 'watch' or 'be alert' – *blepete* and *gregoreo* – is needed at this point. Timothy J. Geddert argues that these two words must not be seen as synonyms and that 'if their function is analysed in the gospel of Mark they can be seen to have very different functions'.[93]

---

[93] Timothy J. Geddert, *Watchwords: Mark 13 in Markan Eschatology* (Sheffield: JSOT Press, 1989), 19.

The parable begins with the imperative *blepete*, literally 'look', or often translated 'be on guard'. This word 'look' or 'see' has been used by Mark as a verbal thread throughout the gospel. This is part of his rhetorical technique that Malbon calls 'repetition' and 'echoing'.[94]

Geddert argues, 'In every one of its occurrences it focuses on a discernment process that looks past externals.'[95] Earlier key repetitions of the word include Mark 4:12, 24; 5:31; 8:15, 18, 23, 24; 12:14, 38. Particularly telling is its use in Mark 8 where Jesus says, 'Watch out [*blepete*] for the yeast of the Pharisees and that of Herod' (Mark 8:15). These repetitions, echoes and juxtapositions underline that 'discernment', paying attention, watchfulness is a key theme throughout the gospel.

Mark then switches to his other key word, *gregoreo*, in the rest of the parable, using it three times (Mark 13:34, 35, 37). He begins the parable with 'look' and ends with 'watch'.

The fact that these two words are brought together in the same parable is significant. It suggests that there is a connection between them, although the fact that Mark switches from one to the other also suggests that Geddert is right when he argues these two words are 'functionally distinct' and not to be seen as synonyms.[96]

I have touched on my view already that watchfulness is to do with being a disciple and watching our heart and mind, because in our hearts and minds we would rather follow our human inclinations than do the things of God.

Our watchfulness is heightened and the fullest revelation is available at the cross. In Mark 15:40, as Jesus suffers on the cross, we are told, 'Some women were watching [*theōrousai*]

---

[94] E. S. Malbon, *In the Company of Jesus: Characters in Mark's Gospel* (Louisville: Westminster John Knox Press, 2000), 18.

[95] Geddert, *Watchwords*, 81.

[96] Geddert, *Watchwords*, 85.

from a distance.' They are closer than the male disciples who have run away, but we need to get close to the cross, not watch it from a distance.

Jesus begins Mark's gospel with a call to repentance (Mark 1:15), because the kingdom has come near. Nowhere is the kingdom nearer than at the cross. The key word, which could be said to provide the plumb line and central idea for all the others, occurs in Mark 1:15 and is the word μετανοεῖτε, usually translated 'repent'. Unfortunately, modern evangelical concepts are often imported into this word and so its importance can be missed. Joel Marcus comments on the word in his *Anchor Bible Commentary*, that literally it means 'change of mind' and implies 'a total change in spiritual orientation.'[97] It is not a one-off conversion-type experience. The tense here is imperative and present continuous: we are to go on having our mind transformed. It is the plumb line because it could be said to be the central intention of Jesus' ministry and the kingdom of God to bring about this total change in spiritual orientation, which could be conceptualised as reperceiving.

That new mind, that complete spiritual reorientation, occurs when we focus our attention on the cross.

---

[97] Marcus, *Anchor Bible Commentary* (2000), 150.

Reflection

Intention

This week, have a daily intention to work on times of silence and solitude.

Attention

How do you look at people? Is it often judgemental? Work on cultivating looking at people with fresh eyes, as if you have never seen them before, and as if you are looking through Jesus' eyes.

Attitude

Our attitude needs to become non-judgemental and compassionate, and about bringing people and our thoughts about them into the light of God's presence.

Chapter six
Jesus as Sage

Read Mark 12:28-34.

Jesus was a prophetic sage.[98] That means His wisdom statements and actions also had prophetic force, the power of speech-acts. He was both influenced by His Jewish heritage and free to demonstrate His uniqueness. Witherington points out that 'Jesus lived at a time when the rivers of the prophetic, apocalyptic, and sapiential traditions had already flowed together'.[99] Jesus drew from all of these traditions but made them His own.

Background

Some background is helpful, as it enables us to see how Jesus was definably different from His contemporaries. Mark's gospel also has some important insights. It is full of the language of perception, and Jesus makes perceiving correctly a central part of His prophetic wisdom, wisdom that is about transforming us as disciples.

What marks Jesus out as a sage is His use of parables (*meshalim* in the Hebrew). I will focus on why He chose to use

---

[98] Ben Witherington III, *Jesus the Sage: The Pilgrimage of Wisdom* (Edinburgh: T & T Clark, 1994), 203.
[99] Witherington III, *Jesus the Seer*, 291.

parables as His primary method of teaching in the next chapter, 'Jesus as Storyteller'.

Wisdom plays a big part of Jesus' teaching, Witherington says that at least '70% of the Jesus tradition is in the form of some sort of Wisdom utterance.'[100] Why is this?

Wise seeing

Part of Jesus' wisdom for us as disciples is that we have to understand that we don't see or hear clearly at a spiritual level, and this is something that needs to change. Jesus outlines the importance of this in Mark 8:17-18 where He says to the disciples, 'Do you still not see or understand? Are your hearts hardened? Do you have eyes but fail to see, and ears but fail to hear? And don't you remember?'

We have already looked at these verses, but Jesus here is saying that our perceptive faculties need to be transformed, our hearts need to be softened (because hard hearts are blind hearts), and we need to develop the capacity to remember prophetically. This is at the heart of His wisdom message. Again, we can make this part of our overall *intention* to transform the way we see, so that we can develop a wise aspect to it.

This transformation of our perceptive faculties, including our spiritual eyes and ears, enables us to reperceive the world and the kingdom hidden within it. As they are transformed we can begin to notice hitherto invisible details, whether in Scripture or our own life. As we notice slivers of change within, flakes of kingdom gold become part of our being, then the gleam of encouragement and faith can be burnished.

It also has another key result.

---

[100] Witherington III, *Jesus the Sage*, 156.

As I have already outlined in the chapter on watchfulness, one of the main themes of Mark's gospel is to stay on the way of the cross as disciples. This is a path of wisdom and ethical living as well as following in the footsteps of Jesus. If our perceptive faculties are transformed, we can learn to act wisely and prophetically in the moment. In the ethical moment of choice we are always faced with a decision either to follow human things or to follow the thing(s) of God (Mark 8:33).

If we find a prophetic, wise state of mind we are more likely to *remember* to choose the things of God. Interestingly, psychology says that we enter a wise state of mind when thinking and feeling minds come together. Here we are saying we enter a prophetically wise state of mind when thinking, feeling and the Holy Spirit come together.

Watchful wisdom

This can be seen as a form of watchful wisdom. Wisdom requires us to develop our attention and awareness. In Proverbs 4, which is all about obtaining wisdom at any cost, we read, 'My son, pay *attention* to what I say; turn your ear to my words. Do not let them out of your sight, keep them within your heart' (Proverbs 4:20-21, italics added).

Seeking wisdom is a form of watchfulness, as in Proverbs 8:34: 'Blessed are those who listen to me, *watching* daily at my doors, waiting at my doorway' (italics added). Indeed, Proverbs 4:6 says, 'Do not forsake wisdom, and she will protect you; love her and she will *watch* over you' (italics added).

What is important to underline here is that Jesus doesn't commend or command any forms of fearful watchfulness. Even when we are arrested and brought to trial for being Christians, He says, 'Do not worry beforehand about what to say. Just say whatever is given you at the time, for it is not you speaking, but the Holy Spirit' (Mark 13:11). As we know, 'the Spirit God gave us does not make us timid, but gives us power, love and self-discipline' (2 Timothy 1:7).

Jesus came to set us free from slavery (Mark 10:45), including the slavery to fear. Romans 8:15 reminds us of this gospel truth: 'The Spirit you received does not make you slaves, so that you live in fear again; rather, the Spirit you received brought about your adoption to sonship.' In that adoption we live in the love that drives out fear, and are able to cry, '*Abba*, Father' (Romans 8:15). And so our *attitude* is constantly to move out of fear into love.

Our well-being

Jesus as a sage was not ascetic in the way some of the desert sages were, and He does not want us to punish or ignore our bodies either. If we are to see clearly, it helps to look after ourselves and our well-being. Jesus models incarnated grace for us. Our *attitude* towards our own embodied self is one of grace, as Jesus said, 'Love your neighbour as yourself' (Mark 12:31).

Incarnated grace

The grace of the Incarnation means we can look for the incarnation of grace in the embodied world in which we live. This grace is incarnated in different ways, including the embedding of wisdom into the natural world.

Grace is often incarnated but unlooked for in the ordinary. It wasn't until the ordinary was temporarily under threat in my own life that I rediscovered this truth.

A while back, a joint in my back jammed, causing a band of muscles to go into spasm and probably pinch a nerve momentarily. For two weeks I couldn't sit up or walk without help. I needed help to get dressed and to wash. Every time I tried to sit up or stand up, my back would spasm again, and I would be literally screaming in pain. I later discovered that I had also suffered an annular tear in one of the discs in my lower back.

Suddenly, in the moment, those ordinary, taken-for-granted experiences, such as sitting, walking and taking a shower, seemed to be wonderful, mysterious things filled with grace and glory. I longed to be able to do them without pain, and to really appreciate them.

How can we remember to appreciate the grace that dwells in ordinary things? By indwelling our grace-given embodied awareness. This embodied awareness is called 'mindfulness' in secular psychology. Mindfulness is our universal human capacity for awareness and attention, and needs to be distinguished from the mindful awareness or meditative practices that enable us to become more mindful.

The gravity of awareness and attention – gravity because it is central to our life and as invisible to us as gravity – is one of the central gifts of grace that is incarnated in our embodied living.

Being mindful

How might we define mindfulness? As we know, the most well-known definition is by Jon Kabat-Zinn: 'Mindfulness means paying attention in a particular way: on purpose, in the present moment, and nonjudgmentally'.[101] This definition can be broken down into the three main components of intention, attention and attitude.[102] *I have already highlighted this, but let's rehearse it again here.*

---

[101] Kabat-Zinn, *Wherever You Go, There You Are*, quoted in Segal, Williams and Teasdale, *Mindfulness-Based Cognitive Therapy for Depression*, 40.

[102] Shapiro et al., 'Mechanisms of Mindfulness', 374.

The purpose of intention is very important. For example, I use secular mindful awareness practices to face my anxiety. I use Christian mindful awareness practices to come into the presence of God, in whose love my fear dissolves. Jesus puts intention at the heart of the attentive life: 'But *seek* first his kingdom and his righteousness, and all these things will be given to you as well' (Matthew 6:33, italics added). Out of our intention comes the motivation to keep seeking, to keep meditating. Bernard of Clairvaux also puts *intentio*, intention, at the heart of the life of prayer. At the heart of *intentio* is the idea of looking closely at God with what Bernard called 'the face of the soul'.[103]

The second key element of mindfulness is attention, which is how we use our awareness. Awareness is 'attending to experience itself, as it presents itself in the here and now.'[104] Jesus also commands us to clearly focus our attention. He does this through stories where we fail to pay attention to the detail: '*Look* at the birds of the air; they do not sow or reap or store away in barns, and yet your heavenly Father feeds them' (Matthew 6:26, italics added). This is not a casual glance but involves *looking* with attention and awareness for the wisdom embedded in the life of these small birds.

Shapiro et al. suggest that the third axiom of mindfulness is attitude. They argue that we can learn to face reality with acceptance, kindness and openness, seeing clearly what is there.[105] Very importantly, they say that this enables us to develop 'the capacity not to continually strive for pleasant experiences, or to push aversive experiences away'.[106]

---

[103] Casey, *Athirst For God*, 117.

[104] Shapiro et al., 'Mechanisms of Mindfulness', 376.

[105] Shapiro et al., 'Mechanisms of Mindfulness', 377.

[106] Shapiro et al., 'Mechanisms of Mindfulness', 377.

Jesus tells us to face the reality of our internal attitudes: 'Why do you look at the speck of sawdust in your brother's eye and pay no attention to the plank in your own eye?' (Matthew 7:3). He also commands us to be non-judgemental and to practise being non-judgemental in a continuous way: 'Do not judge, or you too will be judged' (Matthew 7:1). What He commends is clear seeing: 'First take the plank out of your own eye, and then you will see clearly to remove the speck from your brother's eye' (Matthew 7:5).

Part of wise watching is to listen to the messages our body is sending us. I think I had temporarily got too busy and wasn't paying enough attention to the points of stress in my body, like my back. I am being more attentive now!

Reflection

Intention

Where might you need to intentionally apply wise seeing into your life?

Attention

How do you attend to yourself, compassionately or judgementally and critically?

Attitude

Work this week on moving from fear to love, letting love and compassion be your defining attitude with wise seeing.

Chapter seven
Jesus as Storyteller

Read Mark 12:1-12, and Mark 13:32-37.

The key thing I want to focus on here is why Jesus chose parables as His primary method of teaching. As a prophetic sage, Jesus modelled that He was free from the gravitational pull of the cultural expectations around Him. I believe His primary teaching method of using parables was to enable His listeners to do the same.

Alister McGrath makes the point that a major aspect of Jesus' parables has been neglected, which is the fact that Jesus 'appeals to the world of nature as a means of disclosing the kingdom of God'.[107] This also means that the embodied awareness that observes the world of nature has not been highlighted as a significant factor in Jesus' approach. I believe Jesus inhabited His embodied awareness in a holistic and integrated way, in a way that we have lost in Western culture but was the norm in the Ancient Near East.

You can explore your own embodied awareness by walking attentively in nature. You can also read the new wave of nature writers who use their own highly trained embodied awareness to tell the story of nature. I have found Miriam

---

[107] McGrath, *The Open Secret*, 118.

Darlington and Julian Hoffman particularly helpful in moving me from thinking to awareness.[108]

There is overlap with what I have already said, because *meshalim*, or parables, mark Jesus out as sage. Principally parables, because of the nature of the lyrical and metaphorical language they use, move us out of a place of rational critical thinking into a place of awareness. In this place of awareness we can see what automatic scripts (including cultural ones) are running our lives. The generally received view is that weaving through Mark's gospel is a rhetoric of persuasion. I believe that was not Jesus' *intent*; rather, I believe His intent was much more about helping His listeners to *reperceive* the world, their inner world and the mysterious kingdom that He brought near. His use of parables was intentional, and my view is that He used them as *intentional attentional training tools*. William Sieghart, who founded National Poetry Day here in the UK, wrote recently that scientists at Liverpool University have found that reading the works of Shakespeare and Wordsworth has a 'beneficial effect on the mind, catches the reader's attention and triggers moments of self-reflection'.[109] Let me reflect on that a bit more.

Parables and the lyrical

Within psychology, a very strong argument is being made for the importance of the narrative perspective as part of our self-

---

[108] Miriam Darlington, *Otter Country* (Granta, 2012); Julian Hoffman, *The Small Heart of Things: Being at Home in a Beckoning World* (University of Georgia Press, 2013).

[109] BBC, 'Can poetry really change your life?' Available at http://www.bbc.co.uk/programmes/articles/3JGChfcLw4nyJbkGPDz WTWH/can-poetry-really-change-your-life, accessed 24th November 2015.

understanding. It is, of course, mindless for anything to be automatically assumed to be correct and unquestioned.

Mindfulness as a theory and in its practice does offer another perspective on our self-understanding. In their book, *Teaching Mindfulness*, McCown, Reibel and Micozzi talk about the need for a '*lyric* perspective on self-understanding'.[110] A lyric perspective doesn't define our self-understanding as *who* we are (narrative), but *how* we are; it is about *how* we are in the moment, not *who* we are in a sustained self-story.[111] This can be called our experiential self. I would call it indwelling our embodied awareness.

McCown et al. make the point that this goes against the grain in Western culture, which 'posits the narrative perspective as normative for psychological and moral well-being'.[112] It can be seen, therefore, from this lyric perspective, that mindfulness doesn't just relativise our thoughts; it also relativises our distorted inner narratives, especially those wrapped up in ruminative and secondary emotional processes. Mindfulness asks us to notice these distorted narratives and to let them go. You are bigger than your thoughts, but you are also bigger than your ruminative narratives.

This is not to diminish the importance of narrative but to understand why the lyric perspective on self-understanding – that is, *how* we are and not just *who* we are – is so important. Mindfulness shows us how powerful the narrative perspective is as part of our self-understanding, so we can be *attentive* to our narratives and their distortions, as well as narratives that are more creative and transforming.

---

[110] D. McCown, D. Reibel and M. S. Micozzi, *Teaching Mindfulness* (New York: Springer, 2011), 166.

[111] McCown, Reibel and Micozzi, *Teaching Mindfulness*, 166.

[112] McCown, Reibel and Micozzi, *Teaching Mindfulness*, 166.

Others are also making a plea for the lyric perspective on self-understanding. An example of this is an article by Andrew Abbott, 'Against Narrative: A Preface to Lyrical Sociology'.[113] Part of a lyrical stance is our location in time: 'The lyrical is momentary. This above all is what makes it non-narrative. It is not about something happening. It is not about an outcome. It is about something that is, a state of being.'[114] Such a stance requires a mindful approach.

Another aspect of a lyrical approach is that 'A lyrical writer aims to tell us of his or her intense reaction to some portion of the social process seen in a moment.'[115] This is also part of being mindful.

With its emphasis on paying attention to the present moment, mindfulness invites us to take up this lyric stance to self-understanding. In fact, all mindful awareness practices invite us into this stance. Another way this is done more explicitly is through the use of lyric poetry as a teaching vehicle within mindfulness approaches.[116]

Why this use of lyric poetry might work is explained in Daniel Siegel's book *The Mindful Brain*. The author talks about the mindful awareness induced by [lyric] poetry, creating what he calls 'a receptive presence of mind'.[117] About 'presence' he says, 'I mean quite specifically the state of receptive awareness of our open minds to whatever arises as it arises'.[118] Siegel argues that such poems activate the streams of

---

[113] Andrew Abbott, 'Against Narrative: A Preface to Lyrical Sociology', *Sociological Theory* (2007), 25(1).

[114] Abbott, 'Against Narrative', 75.

[115] Abbott, 'Against Narrative', 76.

[116] I am using 'lyric' here in the sense of being in the moment, an episode rather than a long narrative which lyrical poems can move us into.

[117] Siegel, *The Mindful Brain*, 161 (my brackets and insertion).

[118] Siegel, *The Mindful Brain*, 161.

awareness within us.[119] We are apparently accessing the right hemisphere of our brain when we come across lyrical or ambiguous language. We are often dismissive of the importance of this approach, with a cultural and church emphasis on rational critical thinking which can dominate our life. Our shift in *attitude* is to be receptive rather than dismissive.

Another way to say this is that lyric poetry enables us to shift from the mental gear of *doing* to the mental gear of *being*.

It is not just lyric poetry which can help this process. There is also the constructive use of ambiguous language through creative metaphors, riddles, paradoxical stories and other techniques in Acceptance and Commitment Therapy (ACT). These enable people to see how conditioned their thinking is, with such evocative names as Tin-Can Monster, Feeding the Tiger and the Polygraph metaphor. Another way to put this is to say that these strategies enable cognitive defusion. Cognitive defusion is the term that ACT uses to talk about how we need to realise that our thoughts are not a direct readout of reality, how we need to move to looking *at* our thoughts rather than looking *from* our thoughts.[120]

A more defused thought is when we are able to say, 'I am having the feeling that I am anxious,' rather than a fused thought: 'God, I am so anxious.'[121] Defused thoughts help people to realise how unworkable are their existing strategies for coping.

Someone else who helped people access their lyric stance to self-understanding through mindful riddles, called parables, was Jesus of Nazareth. Dodd defines a parable as 'a metaphor

---

[119] Siegel, *The Mindful Brain*, 162.

[120] S. C. Hayes, *Get Out of Your Mind and Into Your Life* (Oakland: New Harbinger Publications, 2005), 70

[121] Hayes, *Get Out of Your Mind and Into Your Life*, 70.

or simile drawn from nature or common life, arresting the hearer by its ... strangeness, and leaving the mind in sufficient doubt about its precise application to tease it into actual thought'.[122] I would change this to say that the mind is teased into awareness, and is allowed to cognitively defuse from an automatically held position. For example, in the parable of the Good Samaritan, the hearers are cognitively fused to the idea that any Samaritan is a bad person and a non-neighbour. The parable enables some to see that thought, or attitude, in a new light.

A new exodus into freedom

In His parables, Jesus partially exposes the truth to our awareness through the use of paradox, riddle and ambiguity, and allows our awareness to expose the rest of the truth, to use an analogy from photography.

We should not stand over Jesus' parables and pick them to bits; we should go back to them, as if for the first time, staying with them until the truth is exposed by our awareness. Or we can take the principle and rewrite it into our own parables.

Too often we read the parables of Jesus aggressively, trying to pick them apart looking for truth and knowledge. If we read them mindfully, allowing them to dwell in our being, then truth begins to emerge.

As we encounter parables and parables encounter us, then we journey on the way of the new exodus to freedom that Jesus came to bring.

---

[122] Quoted in J. R. Donahue, 'Jesus as the Parable of God in the Gospel of Mark', *Interpretation* XXXII No. 4 (October 1978), 376.

Reflection

Intention

Focus on taking on board Jesus' intention for us, to help us reperceive the world.

Attention

Pay attention over the next few days to becoming aware of your own distorted narratives, as well as more creative and transformative ones.

Attitude

Be receptive and not dismissive of your own inner experience and external circumstances.

Chapter eight
The Desert Sages, Seers, and watchfulness

Read Mark 1:9-16.

In 2006 when I was studying counselling and psychotherapy at Roehampton University, I was very stressed and close to burnout, close to snapping like an overwound violin string. At the same time I was exploring the Christian contemplative tradition, and especially the ancient Christian breath prayer, the Jesus Prayer: 'Lord Jesus Christ, Son of God, have mercy on me, a sinner.'

One of the pioneers of this prayer was a fifth-century Greek Bishop called Diadochus of Photike. A particular phrase of his energised my research into watchfulness and mindfulness from that point on: 'Let us keep our eyes always fixed on the depths of our heart with an unceasing mindfulness of God.'[123]

It was the first time I had heard the phrase 'mindfulness of God', which is a Christian distinctive.

In the contemplative tradition, the Jesus Prayer is a form of 'watchfulness'. In *The Philokalia*, a collection of contemplative texts from the early Christian tradition, the following comment is made about these spiritual writings: 'They show the way to awaken and develop attention and consciousness, to attain that state of watchfulness which is the hallmark of

---

[123] Quoted in Olivier Clement, *The Roots of Christian Mysticism*, 204.

sanctity.'[124] And yet in the twenty-first century, watchfulness does not feature in discussion of discipleship, when once it was at the centre.

One of the reasons for this central place accorded to watchfulness is probably that these early contemplatives were saturated in the Word of God, through *Lectio Divina*, the mindful or meditative reading of Scripture. Reading the early contemplatives took me back to the Bible and the passages that they read, including Deuteronomy, the Psalms and the gospels as well as Paul's letters. *The early contemplatives, including the Desert Sages and Seers (both men and women), said as part of their prophetic wisdom that followers of Christ need to deal with their afflictive thoughts. In fact, we cannot have prophetic insight in a mature way unless we deal with our afflictive thoughts. I will say more about this later in this chapter, particularly with reference to early contemplative and psychologist Evagrius* (AD 345–399).

Watchfulness was a command of Jesus not only to the disciples then, but to disciples now: 'What I say to you, I say to everyone: "Watch!"' (Mark 13:37). This is an imperative, with the sense of continuing to be watchful in the present – it is an ongoing thing. Our *intention* here then can be to decide to deal with, face and address our afflictive thoughts.

The early contemplatives also took seriously Paul's command in 1 Thessalonians 5:17 to 'pray continually'. They realised this could not be endless intercession, but rather a form of watchfulness.

This paying attention as the centre of discipleship also appears in Philippians, in one of the most famous sections: Philippians 2:5-11. One of the key verses is the preceding verse – verse 4 – which is sometimes translated (beginning towards

---

[124] G. E. H. Palmer, P. Sherrard and K. Ware (eds.), *The Philokalia* (London: Faber & Faber, 1979), 13.

the end of verse 3), 'In humility value others above yourselves, not looking to your own interests but each of you to the interests of others.' As we have seen, Stephen E. Fowl in his commentary on Philippians translates it, 'Do not attend to your own interest but rather to the interests of others.'[125]

In the parable of the seed and the sower, which is Jesus' central parable in Mark's gospel, the good soil is the 'attentive listener'.

It could also be argued that watchfulness within the monastic tradition includes systematic self-observation and self-reflection.

This teaching on watchfulness within the contemplative monastic tradition is based on watchfulness in the gospels as well as other scriptures.

Handling afflictive thoughts

One example of a map of the human mind–body system, together with sophisticated investigative tools, is the mature spiritual psychology of Evagrius. The eight afflictive thoughts developed by him are a holistic body–mind–soul examination through self-reflection, illuminated by the Spirit and the Word of God.

According to Andrew Louth, for Evagrius, prayer is 'undistracted attention'.[126] Like all the early contemplatives, he sought to be free of distraction through silence and solitude. It wasn't just outer silence that was required; it was also inner silence, which was much more difficult to find.

---

[125] Fowl, *Philippians*, 77.

[126] Andrew Louth, 'Evagrius on Prayer', in *Stand up to Godwards: Essays in Mystical and Monastic Theology in Honour of the Reverend John Clark on his Sixty-fifth Birthday*, edited by James Hogg (Salzburg: University of Salzburg, 2002), 165.

The inward distractions were chains of thoughts called *logismoi*, which Evagrius put into eight categories: 'gluttony, fornication, avarice, grief (or depression), anger, listlessness (*accidie*, in Middle English), vainglory and pride'.[127]

Bamberger calls this 'psychology of a practical, experiential kind'.[128] We see the examination through self-reflection: 'Let him keep careful watch over his thoughts. Let him observe their intensity, their period of decline and follow them as they rise and fall.'[129] It was to be a non-elaborative awareness with the aim that you catch the first thought as it appears, before a whole train of thought takes your attention away.[130]

This could be called, as in secular mindfulness, the *self-regulation* of attention, and also the ability to *sustain* one's attention. Drawing on the gospels and other scriptures, the early Christian contemplatives called this *nepsis*, or watchfulness: 'One should always stand guard at the door of one's heart or mind.'[131] I would also call this *prophetic self-examination*.

There was no experiential avoidance in this method. Not only were thoughts to be disclosed to a spiritual mother or father, but each thought was named for what it was: anger, lust, greed and so on. All this requires one to be aware in the present moment, without thoughts being suppressed. This watchfulness has an ethical and community dimension.

---

[127] Louth, 'Evagrius on Prayer', 166.

[128] Evagrius Ponticus, *The Praktikos: Chapters on Prayer*, translated by John Eudes Bamberger OCSO (Spencer, Massachusetts: Cistercian Publications, 1970), lxviii.

[129] Evagrius Ponticus, *The Praktikos*, 29.

[130] Mary Margaret Funk, *Tools Matter for Practicing the Spiritual Life* (New York: Continuum, 2004), 53.

[131] Irenee Hausherr, *Spiritual Direction in the Early Christian East*, translated by Anthony P. Githiel (Cistercian Publications, 1990), 225.

The Desert Fathers and Mothers also recognised thoughts as passing events in the mind, rather than a direct readout of reality. Some were harder to deal with than others: 'One should not ask questions about all the thoughts that are [in your mind]; they are fleeting, but [ask] only about the ones that persist and wage war on man.'[132]

The contemplatives, like modern secular psychologists, were aware of our human patterns of either over-engaging and ruminating about thoughts, or avoidance, where we show aversion to the painful experience. The afflictive thought of *acedia*, listlessness, characterises this aversion. Dealing with these thoughts, paying them our *attention* without avoidance, is not selfish but the way through self-centredness.

The aim of watchfulness was to achieve *diakrisis* – 'the seeing clearly into oneself'.[133] *Diakrisis* could lead to *diorasis* or discernment, and one could become a *diaratikos*, a 'Discerning One' – one could say a 'Mindful One'.[134]

Mindfulness of God became the new compass direction for inner transformation. This phrase was used by fifth-century Bishop Diadochus of Photike. The Greek phrase Diadochus uses, which was translated 'mindfulness of God', was *mneme theou*, literally 'the memory of God', or 'the remembrance of God' – a living memory.

When I first read this phrase, 'mindfulness of God', it was like a bell that summoned me towards God; it was like nectar to a bee. Something in me – in fact, of all of me – responded to it. I was directed there by the grace of God. I had forgotten to be mindful of God, and that He was mindful of me.

---

[132] Barsanuphius quoted in Irenee Hausherr, *Spiritual Direction in the Early Christian East*, 227-228.

[133] Funk, *Tools Matter for Practicing the Spiritual Life*, 136.

[134] Hausherr, *Spiritual Direction in the Early Christian East*, 91.

The practice of the memory of God helps us to remember God, to remember others, to remember creation *and* to remember our true self – made in the image and likeness of God. It releases us from the prison of the ego, the ego that sets us in concrete, into a new freedom.

In *The Spirituality of the Christian East*, Tomas Spidlik calls this discernment, this seeing in depth, a charism of the Holy Spirit, which included an ability to see into the hearts of people. It also included knowledge of the mysteries of God.[135] This meant that these early contemplatives were approached for prophetic guidance by others. Talking about spiritual direction in the early Christian East, Irenee Hausherr outlines the importance of this guidance by an *abba*, a spiritual father (there were spiritual mothers as well, *ammas)*. What the disciple would say to the *abba* was, 'Speak a word to me.'[136] This word could be seen as a prophetic portrait of what could be, and what needed to be, transformed.

These words had power. Hausherr points out that 'the spiritual father heals by his *words'*.[137] Here the *attitude* was one of facing reality, our human frailty and God's transforming power. Not only do we need to restore such prophetic insight to the church as a whole, to all believers, but I believe we also need to move away from the cult of celebrity that often surrounds 'prophets', and move away from treating prophetic shows almost as entertainment.

The prophetic needs to be brought back into a relational setting, and we need to grow wise and mature spiritual *abbas* and *ammas* who speak healing words. I have experienced this

---

[135] Tomas Spidlik, *The Spirituality of the Christian East*, translated by Anthony P. Githiel (Collegeville, Minnesota: Liturgical Press, 1986), 77.

[136] Hausherr, *Spiritual Direction in the Early Christian East*, xiii.

[137] Hausherr, *Spiritual Direction in the Early Christian East*, xiii.

wise relational guidance from leaders who are Spirit-bearers, especially within the New Wine network. In particular, this has been in a small group of leaders who meet monthly, built around a spiritual *abba* (and my wife goes to one built around a spiritual *amma*).

What has been particularly important is that the person leading the group has modelled stability in terms of leading a Spirit-filled life, consistently exercising charismatic gifts. As with mindfulness and remembering to be mindful, it is *remembering* to consistently exercise the spiritual gifts we have been given that is difficult.

One modern example of this prophetic healing and wholeness can be seen through the 'sound portraits' that Epiphany, an ensemble of Christian musicians, improvise around someone who is sitting among them as they play. I can see this having a profound prophetic impact on that person, as they are truly heard in all their potential and that 'hearing' is put into a 'sound portrait'.[138]This is an example of the creativity that can be released in the whole area of the prophetic.

As well as exercising spiritual gifts in small groups, the local church must not lose this in its weekly services. Once a month we have been experimenting with what we call an Open Book service, where we have a community *Lectio* on a passage of Scripture and a time of waiting on God to see what emerges, along the lines of the practice of 1 Corinthians 14:26:

> What then shall we say, brothers and sisters? When you come together, each of you has a hymn, or a word of instruction, a revelation, a tongue or an

---

[138] Epiphany Sound Portraits. More information is available at http://epiphanymusic.org.uk/sound-portraits (accessed 18th November 2015).

interpretation. Everything must be done so that the church may be built up.

As I have said elsewhere, scholarship has identified that prophetic words of judgement were few and far between in early Christianity. The main focus seems to have been on spiritual gifts being exercised 'so that the church may be built up'.

Reflection

Intention

Our intention to grow in prophetic insight requires us to intentionally deal with our afflictive thoughts.

What is the thought that afflicts you the most?

Attention

We focus our attention on tracking our afflictive thoughts, so that they might not take us captive. As we witness them, rather than become a victim of them, they are relativised and we can let them go.

Attitude

We face reality and do not avoid painful experiences and thoughts.

Chapter nine
Becoming watchful through Scripture

Read Mark 9:1-13.

At one time, every Christian would pray through a meditative reading of Scripture called *Lectio Divina*. I want to outline the traditional method behind this 'divine reading' before outlining two ways I have used it.

I also need to mention the barriers that some Christians have with reading and praying with Scripture in this way. Some have become so used to just doing Bible study, which can become a way of standing over the text, that they lose sight of the need for the Word to stand over us. Many Christians might agree with memorising Scripture even if they don't do it, but very often the methods for doing this are mechanical and about learning by rote. Through *Lectio* we begin not just to memorise Scripture but also to remember it prophetically, to allow it to dwell within us in a loving, reverential, awe and wonder-filled way.

However, first I need us to revisit our attentional capacities which are at work in this and other spiritual practices. *Lectio Divina* can also be seen as a form of meditation leading to contemplation, and so these two terms need to be defined. Meditation, as we have already discussed, is a form of attentional training. I will say more about this later as it is often misunderstood and feared within some Christian circles, even though it is a biblical concept.

Contemplation is not the same as meditation, although meditation can lead to a contemplative state of mind. The best definition of contemplation I have found is that it is 'an intensification of a transforming awareness of divine presence'.[139]

Focused and distributed attention

The cognitive neuroscience of attention and awareness talks about two attentional processes – focused attention and distributed attention.[140] Focused attention as a process is self-explanatory. Less in our awareness is distributed attention, which is an open awareness to whatever is in the moment. Both are very important. Raffone and his colleagues would argue that these two attentional processes correlate with the two main methods in meditation – focused attention and what they call 'open monitoring'.[141] Mindfulness meditation, for example, often begins with focused attention and leads to open awareness or monitoring.

If we look at the traditional steps of *Lectio Divina*, we can see a similar movement at work.

---

[139] Keith J. Egan, 'Contemplation', in *The New SCM Dictionary of Christian Spirituality*, edited by Philip Sheldrake (SCM Press, 2005), 211.

[140] Antonino Raffone, Angela Tagini and Narayanan Srinivasan, 'Mindfulness and the Cognitive Neuroscience of Attention and Awareness', *Zygon* 45, no. 3 (September 2010), 627-645.

[141] Raffone et al., 'Mindfulness and the Cognitive Neuroscience of Attention and Awareness', 633.

Traditional *Lectio Divina*

There are four movements traditionally in *Lectio*. Christopher Jamison summarises these as 'reading, meditation, prayer and contemplation' (in the Latin, *lectio, meditatio, oratio* and *contemplatio*).[142]

In the reading and the meditation we focus our attention, using both an attentional process and a meditative technique. The reading needs to be slow. With regard to the prayer, I would argue that this should be prophetic, having listened to God first. Contemplation is the place of stillness and awareness of God's presence, in a way that is intensified. This uses the attentional process of open awareness as well as being a skill that can be cultivated.

What is important to say in *Lectio Divina*, as with the Jesus Prayer, is that these are not mechanical techniques; they are part of being in a relationship. Because they can be seen as meditative (or mindful awareness) practices, we need to clear up one particular myth about meditation.

Am I trying to empty my mind in meditation?

One of the biggest myths about mindfulness is that in mindfulness meditation you are trying to empty your mind. Ruby Wax, who is good at answering people's questions, responds to this in her book *Sane New World*: 'It can never be empty while you're alive, even in a coma your mind is still chattering away.'[143]

Why can she and others hold this position so categorically? It is largely to do with how we perceive and define the mind.

---

[142] Abbot Christopher Jamison, *Finding Sanctuary: Monastic Steps for Everyday Life* (Pheonix, 2006), 65.

[143] Ruby Wax, *Sane New World* (London: Hodder & Stoughton, 2013), 136.

Interpersonal neurobiologist Daniel Siegel points out that there is a lack of awareness and understanding of the mind. He defines the mind to be 'a process that regulates the flow of energy and information'.[144] The mind is always receiving information from a great many sources. This includes sources outside of our own self and body. So it isn't possible to empty it.

While not directly addressing the question, 'Am I trying to empty my mind in mindfulness meditation?' Mark Williams looks at mindfulness and psychological processes. He says there are two modes in which the mind operates. These are sometimes called being and doing, but more technically they are 'conceptual (language-based) processing versus sensory-perceptual processing'.[145] Again, that's a lot of information coming into your mind from different sources.

Just picture all the stimuli your senses are sending you from your experience (sometimes called your experiential self), and then all the thoughts that appear in your mind from your narrative or conceptual self!

Our minds are very busy! Now, in a very important and technical phrase, Williams defines what attentional training (mindfulness meditation or mindful awareness practice) is doing, in enabling a shift from doing to being, from thinking to awareness: we learn 'to hold *all* experience (sensory and conceptual) in a wider awareness that is itself neither merely sensory nor conceptual'.[146]

This shift from doing to being, from the narrative self (conceptual mode) to the experiential self (sensory-perceptual

---

[144] Siegel, *The Mindful Brain*, 5.

[145] J. Mark G. Williams, 'Mindfulness and Psychological Process', *Emotion* 10, no.1 (2010): 2. Available at http://dx.doi.org/10.1037/a0018360 (accessed 18th November 2015).

[146] Williams, 'Mindfulness and Psychological Process', 2.

mode), is followed by an ability to hold both in an open, wider awareness. Far from trying to empty our mind, we are learning how to pay attention to all these streams of information, as well as 'our *reactions* to them'.[147]

Why this is important is another question. But staying with the rumour or myth that in mindfulness meditation I am trying to empty my mind, it can also be addressed by approaching it from the angle of feelings and emotion.

In an important article, Rimma Teper addresses this question directly.[148] Mindfulness enables us to monitor, to become aware and to name our subtle emotional experiences.[149] In mindfulness your mind does not work against your embodied mindful brain, but with it!

Mark Williams makes a similar point: 'Mindfulness is not about "not feeling" or becoming detached from affect.'[150] What mindfulness enables is to see 'something *as* it is'.[151]

So are we trying to empty our minds in mindfulness meditation? No, we are not! It may be that in switching to awareness our minds suddenly may feel more spacious, but we are not emptying our minds; rather, we are looking clearly at what our minds are processing. Mindfulness is seeing clearly and feeling clearly. It is an embodied, relational awareness that faces reality; it does not try to avoid it.

---

[147] Williams, 'Mindfulness and Psychological Process', 2.

[148] Rimmer Teper, Zindel V. Segal, and Michael Inzlicht, 'Inside the Mindful Mind: How Mindfulness Enhances Emotion Regulation Through Improvements in Executive Control', *Current Directions in Psychological Science* 22, no. 6 (2013), 449-454: 1, accessed April 5 2015, http://dx.doi.org/10.1177/0963721413495869.

[149] Teper et al., Inside the Mindful Mind', 1.

[150] Williams, 'Mindfulness and Psychological Process', 4.

[151] Williams, 'Mindfulness and Psychological Process', 4.

Attentive reading

Mnemonics are often used in mindfulness training, and I have adapted one of them because the word 'coal' has deep Christian resonance. We can use the mnemonic COAL for the process of reading slowly. Think of the words you are reading as the living coal of God's Word. Ask the Holy Spirit to breathe on the words and fan them into flame. Breathe on them with the breath of your attention.

- **C** – stands for 'curiosity'. Be passionately and dangerously inquisitive about what you are reading and rereading. In our curiosity we stay with the passage, reading it slowly. We leave a gap of silence between each slow reading.

- **O** – stands for 'openness'. Be completely open to what God might be saying to you in a whisper, in a hint, in a riddle. It is in the slow reading and in the gap that we are opening ourselves up and allowing ourselves to be opened up by the Holy Spirit.

- **A** – stands for 'attentiveness'. Thoughts, feelings and other stories will come into your mind and distract you. Keep coming back to the passage you are reading. In this way you strengthen your ability to be attentive. What does God want you to do today? In this in-between place of the living Word of God, the Holy Spirit links our world to God's world. The Word links us to the person and presence of God. Try to find just the one thing God wants you to do this day – the one thing to pray for.

- **L** – stands for 'live it out'. This is not just about doing, but also about staying in the place of being, which is the heart of contemplation. Come back to the Word during the day. Perhaps memorise one verse.

The final step in the process is to take the word 'coal' to represent the burning, purifying presence of God (Isaiah 6:6) and just rest in that presence in a place of contemplative awareness that is beyond words. This would include a *prophetic self-examination.*

Using the muscle of attention

In a little article on the *Mindful* magazine website, Daniel Goleman highlighted the dance steps of the mind in most meditations: focusing our attention, the mind wandering, noticing that the mind has wandered and what it has wandered to, and removing it from where it has become attached and returning to the focus of attention.[152] Goleman points out that there are four things going on in this dance: focused attention, mind wandering, meta-awareness (noticing your mind has wandered), and detaching from where the mind has wandered and bringing it back.

I noticed that the four steps of this dance begin with four letters that make a mnemonic of two parts, FM & MD.

- **F**ocused attention

- **M**ind wandering

- **M**eta-Awareness, which notices the mind has wandered

- **D**etaching from where the mind has wandered and bringing it back

I don't know what these two sets of initials bring to mind for you. Reflect on them for a moment.

---

[152] Daniel Goleman, 'Meditation: A Practical Way to Retrain Attention', November 2013. Available at http://www.mindful.org/meditation-a-practical-way-to-retrain-attention/ (accessed 18th November 2015).

What they bring to mind for me is this. FM I associate with radio stations and tuning in to them. So the steps of focused attention and mind wandering are about tuning in and out from the frequency of our focus. MD I associate with doctors and healing – a Doctor of Medicine.

The healing of our minds and resculpting of our brains occurs through the steps of exercising our muscle of attention. In meta-awareness we notice our mind has wandered, what it has wandered too, and then we direct (I prefer the word 'direct' to 'detach') our mind back to whatever it is we are focusing on.

This popular explanation of the muscle of attention is based on substantial research. Wendy Hasenkamp argues that focused attention meditation can help develop attentional control, as well as awareness of states such as mind wandering, thus enabling us to direct our attention back to what we are focusing on.[153]

The point of the mnemonic is simply to help us remember the four steps of the muscle of attention.

But I also use the mnemonic in *Lectio*. I focus my attention on the passage of Scripture, reading slowly. My mind wanders. I notice this with meta-awareness, that my mind has wandered and what it has wandered too. I direct my attention back to the passage. As I do this my mind becomes less agitated until I find a contemplative state of mind, a place of open awareness. In that place I become aware of the transforming presence of God that gives me prophetic insight for life.

---

[153] Wendy Hasenkamp et al, 'Mind Wandering and Attention During Focused Meditation: A Fine-grained Temporal Analysis of Fluctuating Cognitive States', *Neuroimage* 59 (2012), 751. Available at http://dx.doi.org/10.1016/j.neuroimage.2011.07.008 (accessed 18th November 2015).

Our *intention* here is to listen obediently to the Word of God. Our *attention* is focused on the ways in which God wants us to change to be like His Son Jesus. Our *attitude* is one of stability: we do this every day and do not avoid the discipline of this spiritual practice.[154]

---

[154] For more on the ideas of stability, Christlike change and listening obedience to God, see the Benedictine vows in Jamison, *Finding Sanctuary*, 116-118.

Reflection

Intention

Listening obediently to the Word of God is not easy. *Lectio* enables us to stand under the Word of God, not over it.

Attention

We have to focus our attention on the ways we need to change and the things that help us change to be more Christlike.

Attitude

Focusing on stability in all our relationships is an important aspect of our attitude. Staying present and open, and practising clear seeing and not being judgemental, is at the heart of this.

Chapter ten
Becoming watchful through contemplation

Read Mark 10:46-52.

It is important to clear up from the beginning that the Jesus Prayer, 'Lord Jesus Christ, Son of God, have mercy on me, a sinner,' is not a mantra. It is a way of focusing our attention on the presence of the Lord Jesus Christ with whom we have a relationship. As we focus our attention and still our wandering mind, we become more openly aware of the presence of God, and enter a contemplative state of mind.

Paul prays in Ephesians 3:17 that 'Christ may dwell in your hearts through faith'. In the Jesus Prayer, this is what we seek to experience – the Christ who dwells in our hearts. But Christ is also to be found in the world, and is transcendent – and so we seek this aspect of Christ as well. As Paul declares in Colossians 1:15-16:

> The Son is the image of the invisible God, the firstborn over all creation. For in him all things were created: things in heaven and on earth, visible and invisible, whether thrones or powers or rulers or authorities; all things have been created through him and for him.

I first came across the Jesus Prayer through the former Bishop of Coventry, Simon Barrington-Ward, and his book *The*

Jesus Prayer.[155] This is an ancient meditative prayer that leads to contemplation, stillness and an open awareness of the transforming presence of God. It is an embodied prayer that emphasises posture and uses our breath: 'Lord Jesus Christ, Son of God' is said on the in-breath, and 'have mercy on me, a sinner,' is said on the out-breath.

I have in the last ten years collected many other books on the prayer, and I was fortunate to have a number of conversations with Bishop Simon about his research into and practice of the prayer. You can read about these in *A Book of Sparks*.[156] I remember Bishop Simon saying that when he prayed for those he was about to confirm he would frequently quietly speak in tongues, and often a life-giving word would be given to him for the young person standing before him. I believe that the Jesus Prayer can also open us to kingdom words that are near, to be given by us to others on behalf of God, who is the giving God.

The pioneers of the Jesus Prayer, with an embodied theology and a healthy understanding of the importance of the breath in Scripture, intuitively came across a truth that cognitive neuroscience has acknowledged more recently. Neuroscience has discovered that 'emotions such as fear, anger, anxiety, and happiness are related to specific breathing patterns'.[157] What this means is that when we attend to our breath, these emotions and the afflictive thoughts that are part of them come into our awareness.

---

[155] Simon Barrington-Ward, *The Jesus Prayer* (Oxford: BRF, 2007).
[156] Lambert, *A Book of Sparks*.
[157] Paul Grossman, 'Mindfulness for Psychologists: Paying Kind Attention to the Perceptible', *Mindfulness* 1, (2010), 92. http://dx.doi.org/10.1007/s12671-010-0012-7 (accessed 21 January 2016).

Of course, the contemplative pioneers very quickly became aware of the difficulty of sustaining attention. As I have already outlined when talking about *Lectio*, the cognitive neuroscience of attention and awareness talks about two attentional processes: focused attention and distributed attention.[158] Focused attention as a process is self-explanatory; less in our awareness is distributed attention, which is an open awareness to whatever is in the moment. Both are very important. Raffone and his colleagues would argue that these two attentional processes correlate with the two main methods in meditation – focused attention and what they call 'open monitoring'.[159] Mindfulness meditation, for example, often begins with focused attention and leads to open awareness or monitoring.

The Jesus Prayer also begins with focused attention and leads to open awareness or monitoring. As we have discussed, Wendy Hasenkamp and others suggest that there is a cycle that goes on in our minds: 'mind wandering, awareness of mind wandering, shifting of attention, and sustained attention.'[160]

Daniel Goleman calls this the muscle of attention, and, as previously mentioned, his four steps are focused attention, mind wandering, the meta-awareness of noticing the mind has wandered and what it has wandered to, and directing it back to whatever is the focus of attention.

The mnemonic I have created for the muscle of attention also works for the Jesus Prayer. Part of being aware and

---

[158] Raffone et al., 'Mindfulness and the Cognitive Neuroscience of Attention and Awareness', 627-645.

[159] Raffone et al., 'Mindfulness and the Cognitive Neuroscience of Attention and Awareness', 633.

[160] Hasenkamp, 'Mind Wandering and Attention During Focused Meditation', 750.

attentive is remembering what is important, and we remember through repetition – which is why I am underlining this again!

- Focused Attention

- Mind wandering

- Meta-awareness, which notices that the mind has wandered

- Detaching (directing) from where the mind has wandered and bringing it back

The Jesus Prayer, as I pray it repeatedly, helps me focus my attention on the presence of God. God's presence is always there; we are just not usually aware of it. Our mind will wander, pulled as it is by the gravity of self-centredness and the concerns of the false self.[161] It can be wandering in mental time travel for some time before meta-awareness picks up that it has wandered and what it has wandered too. Then we direct the focus of our attention back to the Jesus Prayer. The more we exercise the muscle, the longer we can sustain our attention. The longer we can sustain our attention, the easier it is to find the contemplative state of mind that is openly aware of the transformative presence of God. Whenever we use a meditative practice or other form of focused attention to arrive at a contemplative state, an *intention* is to remember to exercise the muscle of attention.

---

[161] Benedictine monk Thomas Keating defines the false self as 'that developed in our own likeness rather than in the likeness of God' and so is particularly self-centred and controlling, see *Open Mind, Open Heart* (New York: Continuum, 2009), 187.

Some more background

At the beginning of this chapter you read the story of blind Bartimaeus. He calls out from the side of the 'way' to Jesus, 'Jesus, Son of David, have mercy on me!' (Mark 10:47). This is prophetic insight, clear seeing from a blind man, and it becomes one of the prayers on which the Jesus Prayer is based. Bartimaeus calls out repeatedly, which is another important principle taken up by the Jesus Prayer.

It is also the type of prayer that Jesus commends in His parable of the Pharisee and the tax collector (Luke 18:9-14). The Jesus Prayer takes up the theme of this parable: 'For all those who exalt themselves will be humbled, and those who humble themselves will be exalted.'

The other connection between the Jesus Prayer and Mark's gospel is that the pioneers of the Jesus Prayer saw it as a way of cultivating watchfulness. Through it we can become free of the gravitational pull of the eight afflictive thoughts identified by Evagrius and others. Instead of being held by these thoughts, we hold them and recognise them as thoughts rather than reality, which relativises them and robs them of power. We can then let them go.

This is just part of the *intention* behind the prayer. It is also about learning to pray continually (1 Thessalonians 5:17), a continuous prayer that is about being attentive and listening to God, not offering endless intercessions.

Diadochus of Photike

Being in the presence of God is dynamic, not static; it is about going on a journey, the way of the Lord. Diadochus of Photike (AD 400–487), who helped pioneer the Jesus Prayer, lays out beautifully the intention behind it. We pray the Jesus Prayer that we might learn to 'follow the footprints of the Invisible One'.[162]

This is why we need to learn to pray contemplatively, because following in the footprints of the Invisible One is not easy; it requires the cultivation of watchfulness, stillness and discernment. Diadochus knows that the beginner on this path 'is not free from a wandering mind'.[163]

The *attitude* is one of humility, as commended by Jesus in His parable of the Pharisee and the tax collector. As we cultivate an awareness of our self-love that is self-centred rather than God-centred, there is a movement towards this greater love: 'Once he has transcended his self-love through love for God, his heart becomes consumed in the fire of love.'[164] But this is not easy; this is tough love at work, not sentimental love. This is why Diadochus chooses a particular word for the person who pursues the path of contemplative prayer, and that word is 'warrior' (*agonistes* in the Greek).[165]

This is what I wrote in *A Book of Sparks* about Jesus as the warrior and how this can help men re-engage with church:

> One of the keys to bringing men back to the kingdom and the church is to rediscover a lost portrait of Jesus: He is not gentle Jesus, meek and mild; He does not float around in a nightgown.
>
> Mark's gospel offers us a neglected title for Jesus, one that speaks powerfully to men. Jesus is called the

---

[162] Diadochus of Photike, *Following the Footsteps of the Invisible: The Complete Works of Diadochus of Photike*, introduction, translation and notes by Cliff Ermatinger (Collegeville, Minnesota: Liturgical Press, 2010), 69.

[163] Diadochus, *Following the Footsteps of the Invisible*, 95.

[164] Diadochus, *Following the Footsteps of the Invisible*, 75.

[165] See Ermatinger's comments on page 15 of his introduction to Diadochus, *Following the Footsteps of the Invisible*.

'one more powerful' by John the Baptist (Mark 1:7). In the Greek He is literally 'the stronger one'.

Who does this make Jesus like? This echoes the portrayal of Yahweh as divine warrior in Isaiah's new exodus theology. Mark's gospel employs the same root Greek word that is used in the Septuagint version of Isaiah 40:10. Yahweh comes with power in that verse, with the sense of being the more powerful one, the stronger one. In Isaiah 49 Yahweh will contend with fierce warriors and take plunder and captives from them.

It is this language that Jesus picks up when He is accused by the teachers of the law of being possessed by Satan: 'By the prince of demons he is driving out demons' (Mark 3:22). Jesus calls them to Him and speaks to them in an important parable.

No one, He says, can 'enter a strong man's house and carry off his possessions unless he first ties up the strong man. Then he can rob [plunder] his house' (Mark 3:27). Satan is the strong man here; it is the same root Greek word which describes Jesus as 'the stronger one'. As the stronger one, Jesus is the divine warrior who has come to bind the strong man and plunder his house and his kingdom.

Jesus bound Satan in His encounter with him in the desert (Mark 1:13), and the first miracle recorded by Mark is the driving out of an evil spirit (Mark 1:21–27). Jesus has already demonstrated the truth of His parable, that He has bound Satan and is now plundering his kingdom.

But it is on the cross that He completes His eschatological victory over Satan, death and sin. Christ the divine warrior as Victor needs to be rediscovered. That victory, won in principle, needs now to be won in reality in the present through hard

conflict. Men who are caught in bitter existential
battles with lust, greed, power and the slavery of the
economic system – who are caught in addictions to
pornography, alcohol, drugs and the emptiness of
competing in the arena of consumerism – need to
hear the language of the strong man being bound in
their lives. This language needs to be part of their
spiritual rebirth. This is a journey out of mindless
living, where we are stuck in automatic thinking, or
in avoidance of our real issues; it is a journey into
self-awareness and mindfulness.[166]

Not only does contemplation help us learn to work with
our wandering mind, but Diadochus goes on to say that it
'frees up [the mind] making it open and expansive.'[167] This is
his early discerning of our God-given capacity for open
awareness, for a contemplative state of mind. This state of
mind can become a trait, part of our character.

We have been talking about Jesus as our model for wisdom
and spiritual gifts, and that we can cultivate these things along
with prophetic insight through watchfulness, *Lectio* and the
Jesus Prayer. Diadochus speaks out of his own experience and
wisdom as a man of prayer when he goes on to say, 'Wisdom
comes through humble meditation of God's word.'[168]

Another person connected with the Jesus Prayer was St
Macarius the Spiritbearer (AD 300–390). What others called
him – 'Spiritbearer' – is what we should all seek to be. It sums
up a person of contemplative prayer – and, of course, the
Spirit is the Spirit of Jesus (Acts 16:7).

What these early Sages and Seers had with this saturation
in the Word of God and the Holy Spirit was an ability to give

---

[166] Lambert, *A Book of Sparks*, 91-92.

[167] Diadochus, *Following the Footsteps of the Invisible*, 101.

[168] Diadochus, *Following the Footsteps of the Invisible*, 73.

life-changing prophetic insights to those who came to learn from them. Focusing our *attention* on these twin tracks of transformation opens up the path of the kingdom for us.

Reflection

Intention

Our intention in this chapter is to remember to cultivate the use of our muscle of attention, in any practice or exercise that requires focused and sustained attention.

Attention

To arrive at transformation into Christlikeness we focus our attention on the twin tracks of the Word and the Spirit.

Attitude

This chapter reminds us of the importance of humility as an attitude. In humility we transcend our self-love without slipping into self-hate.

Chapter eleven
Reading the signs of these times

Reading the signs of these times is a key element of being watchful, of speaking and acting out of mature prophetic insight. We live in a culture in the West that is rewriting the rules. We have often responded with fear as Christians. Instead *we need to respond prophetically, with love, compassion and the clear seeing of truth.*

As a church we have lived out of a 'body bad, spirit good' split, and we need to restore the physical body and embodied awareness to the heart of Christianity. We are an incarnated people.

Harrow, where I live, is one of the most religiously and ethnically diverse boroughs in Western Europe, and the traditional 'come to us' approach of church is not enough as a mission strategy. We need to move towards our neighbours incarnationally. We do this here in Stanmore through a Healing on the Streets (SHOTS) ministry every week and a Mindful Church Café in the local Costa. Both of these are incarnational communities.

What is interesting is that SHOTS has had a prophetic impact as a sign of the kingdom. A number of people have watched from a distance as the team go out every Saturday morning, in snow, rain or sunshine. They may work locally or come in to Stanmore on a Saturday morning to shop in Sainsbury's. After maybe a year of watching they will come and talk to us about what they have seen – whether it is the radiance of the people praying or the radiance of people after they have been prayed for. Often they will then ask for prayer themselves.

Also, as a church, we have recently become a sponsoring agency for visas so that we can explore the possibility of partnering with cross-cultural workers from the USA.

All these possibilities came out of a prophetic vision my wife had, in which she saw a man walking by the church, on the other side of the road. He didn't even know we were there, and even if he had, he wouldn't have entered the church building.

Just as God has had to call those outside the church to be *prophetic* about ecological issues and climate change, so in the area of attention and awareness, of the cultural phenomenon of mindfulness, it is those outside the church who are *prophetically* leading the way. Out of the movement of mindfulness for health, which is backed up by convincing empirical research and neuroscientific evidence, is emerging a strong development of *secular spirituality*.

Based around mindfulness and meditation, this secular spirituality is both an opportunity for and a threat to the church. The reality is that secular mindfulness practices are transformative, transformative enough for some to believe they don't need God. It is not militant atheists who threaten the church; it is the more peaceful secular spirituality that needs to be taken notice of. We need to show that mindfulness of God is a Christian distinctive that offers transformation far beyond the meditations for health that secular psychology rightly offers.

In particular, I have been asking the question, 'How might we mature the prophetic?' The answer is through watchfulness. We develop watchfulness through intention, attention and attitude.

In terms of our *intention*, we are looking closely at being Spirit-bearers every day, who are in the presence of Jesus each moment of our life. We intentionally practise spiritual disciplines like silence, solitude, the slow meditative reading of Scripture *(Lectio Divina)* and the Jesus Prayer. As we become contagiously holy with the presence of Jesus and are filled with insight, faith, clear seeing and prophetic embodied feelings of wonder and awe, we may enable others to 'catch' this magnetic holy presence of Jesus. Again, we are not pointing to ourselves but away from ourselves, pointing to someone greater, as John the Baptist did.

In order to become spiritual we need to re-inhabit our bodies and intentionally 'come to our senses'. As we do so (and remember I have suggested there are nine senses), we enter the world of perception and step out of rational critical thinking where we are often stuck, and where it is harder for God to reach us. In each spiritual practice we exercise our muscle of attention, until 'watchfulness' and the prophetic become a state of mind as well as a trait of our character and being. We need to exercise prophetic self-examination, and face and deal with our afflictive thoughts – anger, pride and others – which are all fear based. We focus on the present moment and do not waste time in mental time travel, worrying about a past we cannot change, or a future we cannot control.

Our central intention is the intention that Jesus has for us, which is to become like Him. As we become like Him we learn to reperceive the world and the hidden kingdom within it. We need to take on board the type of *prophetic seeing* that Jesus modelled for us, where we look at people with the eyes of God, seeing them as He sees them. That means a clear seeing that sees their potential in the kingdom, as well as the inclinations that need transforming – but transforming through love, compassion and truth, not through judgementalism.

Training our attention and awareness is at the heart of maturing the prophetic. God looks at us mindfully, with loving attention, remembering us in His being and doing. We are to mirror that in our own lives, made in the image of God as we are.

As we work intentionally with our God-given capacity for attention and awareness, we are seeking to move from a cultural self-focused attention to being attentive to God, others and creation. Our God-given attention and awareness has varying capacities: we can focus our attention, switch our attention, and find distributed or open attention and awareness. We can find states of mind that are attentive in different ways: contemplative, prophetic, still, wise and so on.

The mature prophet and disciple has freed himself or herself from the gravitational pull of our culture; their attention is no longer held captive by the things of this world, is no longer fragmented or distracted. With undistracted attention we can choose the things of God in each ethical moment of choice.

The faith we are called to is a perceptive faith. In it we are cultivating attitudes that help us develop that perceptiveness. When we are fearful and anxious, our capacity to access our wise, still state of mind is limited. In training our attention we are moving from fearful, anxious, self-focused attention, and from acquisitive, competitive attitudes to Christlike ones of kindness, openness, compassion, acceptance, gratitude and humility. Out of humility we need to say, 'I could be wrong.' We also need to check out any insights we have against Scripture, because what the Holy Spirit gives us to share will not contradict God's Word.

This involves a new exodus, a movement from slavery into freedom. In that freedom we can 'imagine and articulate a real historical newness in our situation'.[169]

In terms of the practices that help us develop our prophetic insight, let me say a bit more about that. I would begin with *lectio*, which is how we get the seed of the Word, of the kingdom within. As this grows by God's grace, so does our prophetic insight. In the traditional way of praying the Word (*lectio*), the third movement is prayer (*oratio*), and this can include prophetic words, pictures or any other form of communication from God. The fourth movement is contemplation, and here we have entered a contemplative state of mind in which we can also be open to the prophetic. The good soil in Mark 4:1-9 is the attentive listener. Here we develop 'earsight'.

One of the guiding principles can be the command in 1 Thessalonians 5:17 to 'pray continually'. This is not, as we have said, a command for continuous intercession, but rather for continuous listening, for being in the presence of God all the time. In this sense, prophetic insight can arrive at any time. This is underlined by the idea of the *kairos* moment, the opportune moment – the fact that every moment is pregnant with the possibility of encountering God. This means all time can be redeemed, and can be open to the streams of God's communication to us.

I remember sitting in a worship service with my eyes closed, listening attentively. I felt an arm around my shoulders. It didn't feel invasive; it felt affirming, like the giving of assurance. I looked around and smiled, expecting to see a friend, but no one was there. Just the hand tracks of the Invisible One.

---

[169] Brueggeman, *The Prophetic Imagination*, 39.

God's speaking is traced on our minds, bodies, souls and hearts – it can take the form of feelings, thoughts, bodily sensations, pictures. As we enter prophetic states of mind and these become traits, we become sensitively magnetised to these tracings of light, love and truth. We may experience them as an allusion, an inkling, an echo, a foretaste, a foreshadowing... In this way we become Spirit-bearers, bearers of the reality of Jesus and the kingdom. This is the foundation stone for our own prophetic development.

We face reality with embodied grace, and from a place of stability, not being caught up in the experiential avoidance or compliance that marks so much of Western culture. It is interesting that God often raises up prophetic leaders to challenge the powers and authorities of culture, people such as Gandhi, Martin Luther King Jr, Nelson Mandela, who speak and act with grace and truth rather than rhetoric.

In a similar vein, which I have touched on in terms of taking the prophetic out of the realm of celebrity and performance, is to pick up the theme of secrecy in Mark's gospel. For example, at the end of the story of the raising of Jairus' daughter from the dead, it says in 5:43, 'He gave strict orders not to let anyone know about this, and told them to give her something to eat.' Marshall comments perceptively that this 'represents an attempt by Jesus to discourage a popular following based on external wonders and divorced from genuine repentance and faith'.[170] There needs to be more of a 'secrecy' motif in the modern church. If we can take prophecy out of the realm of celebrity and performance and give it back to the ordinary followers of Jesus in each congregation, then once again it can lead people to genuine repentance and faith, rather than just attract a popular following built around celebrity prophets.

---

[170] Marshall, *Faith as a Theme in Mark's Narrative*, 99.

As a child I had a chameleon. I would watch, fascinated, as it blended in with its surroundings, able to perceive the exact hues around it and mimic them. It did this out of physical stillness, holding a branch, only occasionally moving in its strange, alien, jerky way. As Christians we are able to do something similar. But in the places we stand we are not to blend in with the cultural palette around us (although we often do), but to attune ourselves to the colours of the hidden kingdom in that place – and so to stand out, to be a witness to another way, a different path. This is our prophetic witness.

> May the full magnetic
> Tracing of God's light, love, truth
> Remake you wakeful.

A study guide for leaders and participants using *Putting on the Wakeful One* as a six-week course

I am hoping that a number of churches and small groups will use *Putting on the Wakeful One* as a resource for a six-week course. I have produced this study guide, which will enable anyone reading the book or leading a small group to run a course to introduce 'Attuning to the Spirit of Jesus through watchfulness'. I have also recorded six podcasts that are available at http://shaunlambert.co.uk/podcasts/. These are a good introduction to mindfulness, awareness and attention, and I am looking to record some more specifically for this book. Do check my website for the ones specifically for this book, which will be designed to be used individually or in a group with this study guide.

Slow reading of *Putting on the Wakeful One*

Encourage everyone to read two chapters a week, slowly and with *attention*, and to do the spiritual practices suggested. Invite people to come back to the section in the introduction on mindful reading, until the principles become part of them. Each week you can do a *Lectio*, which is one of the principal ways we develop our prophetic insight.

Paying attention wherever we are

The book looks at different aspects of developing prophetic insight to help us pay attention wherever we are.

Other resources

At the end of the study guide, I will suggest other resources to help people engage. These include a radio interview, helping men engage, and drawing out the often hidden creative gifts people have for poetry, art and so on, which can also be used to develop prophetic insight. Many of these resources can be printed.

Preparation

We are tracking some of the journey of Jesus and the disciples from the beginning of the gospel through to the cross and resurrection. It is our journey too.

Mark's gospel was originally an oral gospel, to be listened to as a whole, not just read. We have found that encouraging people to listen to it as a whole, or to long sections, is very helpful. The best 'performance' of it is the DVD of Max McLean's complete rendition on stage.[171]

Suggestions:

- Have an evening where you watch it together.

- Play sections during a Sunday service.

- Encourage house groups to watch it.

---

[171] Available to buy online, or at https://www.youtube.com/watch?v=td3FKGN1AsM (accessed 18th November 2015).

Weekly guide

Week one

I am asking you to read two chapters a week. This week, read the introduction and chapter one, 'Jesus and watchfulness'. Consider the full implication of 'putting on the Wakeful One' for your own life.

Is there any particular aspect of Jesus' character that you need to work on? Can you see the centrality of your spiritual eyes and ears needing to be opened?

Introduction

- Read the section 'Immersing in Scripture' again in the introduction which introduces the psalms as acts of meditation, and have a go at writing your own meditative psalm.

Chapter one: Jesus and watchfulness

- As you look again at this chapter, summarise what it says about watchfulness in all its dimensions. Explain it in your own words, and again seek to apply to your own life (lives).

Week two

This week the two chapters to review are chapters two and three, 'Jesus as Saviour' and 'The attentional capacities we use'.

Chapter two: Jesus as Saviour

- What do you learn about Mark's gospel?

- Reflect some more on the idea of 'perceptive' faith that Mark presents.

Reread this little section, from chapter two:

> In a piece of detail that is often missed as we skim-read Scripture, when Jesus appoints the 12 it is in part that 'they might be with him' (3:14). Part of the transformation that occurs in the disciples, and in all disciples, is when they are in the *presence* of Jesus.[172] In Jesus we come near the kingdom of God. As theologian Hans Kung puts it, 'God's kingdom is creation healed.'[173]

- Are there any stories you can tell yourself, or share with others about being in the presence of Jesus?

- Read Mark 10:45 and reflect on serving and giving in your own life.

Chapter three: The attentional capacities we use

Try a corporate *Lectio Divina*. Read Mark 4:1-9, the parable of the seed and the sower, using the guidance provided in the

---

[172] Watts Henderson, *Christology and Discipleship in the Gospel of Mark*, 4.

[173] *A Time to Heal*, 25.

Lectio (chapter nine). Remind people about the muscle of attention.

Write your own personal rhythm of life that builds in time for silence and contemplation, that enables you to develop prophetic insight through being in the presence of God and listening to God. As well as first thing in the morning, just stepping out of clock time – for one minute or perhaps three minutes – can reconnect you with the presence of God.

Week three

This week we are paying attention to chapters four and five, 'Jesus and the senses' and 'Jesus as Seer'. Coming to our senses and learning to re-inhabit our bodies is crucial in facing our emotions and using these streams of awareness to help us develop our prophetic insight.

Chapter four: Jesus and the senses

- Can you think of a time you experienced embodied awe, reverence, wonder?

- The prophetic Word can impact us with bodily force. Again, can you think of a time this happened to you?

- Whether you are on your own or part of a group, go out for a walk to contemplate and consider 'the works of God's hands' around you.

This is a quote from the section 'Christian Distinctives' in chapter three about how our attention is captured by our culture:

> That we are psychologically captured in terms of our attention (which directs the focus and path of our life) is borne out by all the research into the virtual world in which we live, which includes the loss of deep attention and the rise of the hyper attention I have mentioned already.

- How has your attention been captured?

Chapter five: Jesus as Seer

We are looking to cultivate a character that is Christlike. One of the practices we use with this is self-examination. Take some time out now to memorise through loving repetition 2 Corinthians 13:5: 'Examine yourselves to see whether you are in the faith; test yourselves.' In humility we need to remember that we can be wrong, and that the prophetic insights we are given are provisional and conditional. If they are correct, they will not contradict Scripture.

- Reread the section on 'prophetic seeing' in chapter five on Jesus' prophetic seeing, how He sees people. Examine your own judgemental thoughts when it comes to other people. We cannot give words from God if our default position is one of negativity and criticism towards others.

- Look again at the ideas of embodied actions or signs that are prophetic.

- Look also at prophetic remembering and developing a prophetic state of mind.

Try a *Lectio* now and see if you can access prophetic remembering, and a prophetic state of mind.

Close with a time of silence and solitude, which is another key practice in helping us develop all of the above.

Week four

In week four we are reading chapters six and seven, 'Jesus as Sage, and 'Jesus as Storyteller'. Each of us needs to seek wisdom, and it is a prophetic wisdom, a wise seeing.

Chapter six: Jesus as Sage

- Review what you have learnt so far about Jesus and what He models for us.

- We are called to prophetic transformative language and actions. What are your language and actions communicating?

- Wisdom begins with understanding our own spiritual blindness and deafness. We need the transformation that the kingdom brings in order to reperceive the world and the hidden kingdom within it.

Jesus doesn't model extreme asceticism, but He came to bring wholeness and well-being, as well as resilience in the face of suffering. What is the state of your own well-being?

Chapter seven: Jesus as Storyteller

Do a *Lectio* on one of the kingdom parables, such as Mark 4:21-25.

- Does anything emerge that might be prophetic and transformative?

- Are you able to see the shift from thinking to awareness as you pay attention to it – or are you trying to pull it to bits, as you might pull the petals off a flower?

Reread this summary statement of parables from chapter seven:

There is overlap with what I have already said, because *meshalim*, or parables, mark Jesus out as sage. Principally parables, because of the nature of the lyrical and metaphorical language they use, move us out of a place of rational critical thinking into a place of awareness. In this place of awareness we can see what automatic scripts (including cultural ones) are running our lives. The generally received view is that running through Mark's gospel is a rhetoric of persuasion. I believe that was not Jesus' *intent*; rather, I believe His intent was much more about helping His listeners to *reperceive* the world, their inner world and the mysterious kingdom that He brought near.

Week five

This week we are reviewing chapters eight and nine, 'The Desert Sages, Seers and watchfulness', and 'Becoming watchful through Scripture'.

Chapter eight: The Desert Sages, Seers and watchfulness

Review the ideas of mindfulness of God, clear seeing, and dealing with our afflictive thoughts.

- Have a time of listening to God and see if you can hear the words of healing and wholeness God wants to speak to you or to your group. Try to develop some prophetic portraits for each person in the group.

Chapter nine: Becoming watchful through Scripture

Are there any barriers to praying through a *Lectio* that you can identify for yourself or within the group? These might include misunderstandings about meditation. Review the teaching on this in this chapter.

- Review the definitions of meditation and contemplation.
- Practise some attentional reading, taking up a passage of Scripture.
- Revise what the muscle of attention is.

Week six

This week, read chapters ten and eleven, 'Becoming watchful through Scripture' and 'Reading the signs of these times'.

Chapter ten: Becoming watchful through contemplation

Begin by finding stillness through using the Jesus Prayer, either as an individual or in your group. Review again what you have learnt about the importance of the breath.

- Did anything come into your awareness as you used the embodied breath prayer, 'Lord Jesus Christ, Son of God, have mercy on me, a sinner'?

- The open awareness you are looking to find, which is a state of mind, is also the place you find your God-given creativity. You can be creative or rigid, whatever it is you are doing, whatever work you do, whatever relationships you have.

Chapter eleven: Reading the signs of these times

This chapter is a review of the whole book. It is a good time to look again at some key things:

- What would a perceptive faith look like for you?

- We need to move from cultural self-focused attention and cultural captivity to free attention and awareness that is shaped like Christ.

- As spiritual warriors, we need to persevere as well as imagine new futures. Do that now.

- How can you help each other, or yourself, to live consistently in these practices, and in community?

Perhaps you can text each other a reminder to practise each day.

Bring out the importance of slowing down, and the importance of reclaiming our bodies within our spiritual practice. Emphasise that the cross and resurrection are the place of the fullest revelation for us.

Afterwards

Follow up with a Quiet Day or a retreat for the church.

Other resources[174]

Interview on Premier Radio re mindfulness from a Christian perspective with Shaun Lambert. Available at https://www.premierchristianradio.com/Shows/Weekday/Inspirational-Breakfast/Interviews/Shaun-Lambert-Christian-Mindfulness

An ancient term for a contemplative was a 'tracker' – a word that helps men engage. Available at http://www.instantapostle.com/blog/is-lent-for-men-rediscovering-the-lost-art-of-spiritual-bushcraft/

Three-minute breathing space to help us step out of clock time during a busy day: http://shaunlambert.co.uk/2015/05/27/three-minute-breathing-space-by-the-sea-mindfulness/

More on attention, awareness and mindfulness From Premier Mind & Soul: http://www.mindandsoul.info/Groups/171284/Mind_and_Soul/Resources/Topics/Mindfulness/Mindfulness.aspx

---

[174] All websites in this section accessed 15th November 2015.

Bibliography and suggested reading

Books

Aune, David E. *Prophecy in Early Christianity and the Ancient Mediterranean World*. Grand Rapids, Michigan: William B. Eerdmans Publishing Company, 1983.

Barrington-Ward, Simon. *The Jesus Prayer*. Oxford: BRF, 2007.

Black, C. Clifton. *Mark: Abingdon New Testament Commentaries*. Nashville: Abingdon Press, 2011.

Brock, Sebastian. *The Luminous Eye: The Spiritual World Vision of Saint Ephrem the Syrian*. Kalamazoo, Michigan: Cistercian Publications, 1985.

Brown, Alexandra R. *The Cross and Human Transformation*. Minneapolis: Fortress Press, 1995.

Brown, William P. *Psalms*. Nashville: Abingdon Press, 2010.

Brueggeman, Walter. *The Prophetic Imagination*, second edition. Minneapolis: Fortress Press, 2001.

Casey, Michael. *Athirst For God: Spiritual Desire in Bernard of Clairvaux's Sermons on the Song of Songs*. Kalamazoo: Cistercian Publications, 1988.

Clement, Olivier. *The Roots of Christian Mysticism*. London: New City, 2002.

Darlington, Miriam. *Otter Country*. Granta, 2012.

Diadochus of Photike. *Following the Footsteps of the Invisible: The Complete Works of Diadochus of Photike*. Introduction, Translation and Notes by Cliff Ermatinger, Collegeville, Minnesota: Liturgical Press, 2010.

Edwards, James R. *The Gospel According to Mark: The Pillar New Testament Commentary*. Leicester: Apollos, 2002.

Evagrius Ponticus. *The Praktikos: Chapters on Prayer*. Translated by John Eudes Bamberger OCSO. Spencer, Massachusetts: Cistercian Publications, 1970.

Fowl, Stephen E. *Philippians: The Two Horizons New Testament Commentary*. Grand Rapids, Michigan: William B. Eerdmans Publishing Company, 2005.

France, R. T. *The Gospel of Mark: The New International Greek Testament Commentary*. Grand Rapids, Michigan: William B. Eerdmans Publishing Company, 2002.

Funk, Mary Margaret. *Tools Matter for Practicing the Spiritual Life*. New York: Continuum, 2004.

Garrett, Susan R. *The Temptations of Jesus in Mark's Gospel*. Grand Rapids, Michigan: William B. Eerdmans Publishing Company, 1998.

Geddert, Timothy J. *Watchwords: Mark 13 in Markan Eschatology*. Sheffield: JSOT Press, 1989.

Hausherr, Irenee. *Spiritual Direction in the Early Christian East*. Translated by Anthony P. Githiel. Cistercian Publications, 1990.

Hayes, S. C. *Get Out of Your Mind and Into Your Life*. Oakland: New Harbinger Publications, 2005.

Hayles, N. Katherine. *How We Think: Digital Media and Contemporary Technogenesis*. Chicago: The University of Chicago Press, 2012.

Henderson, Suzanne Watts. *Christology and Discipleship in the Gospel of Mark.* Cambridge: Cambridge University Press, 2006.

Hoffman, Julian. *The Small Heart of Things: Being at Home in a Beckoning World.* University of Georgia Press, 2013.

Jamison, Abbot Christopher. *Finding Sanctuary: Monastic Steps for Everyday Life.* London: Phoenix, 2006.

Kabat-Zinn, Jon. *Wherever You Go, There You Are: Mindfulness Meditation in Everyday Life.* New York: Hyperion, 1994.

Keating, Thomas. *Open Mind, Open Heart.* New York: Continuum, 2009.

Laird, M. *Into The Silent Land.* London: DLT, 2006.

Lambert, Shaun. *A Book of Sparks: A Study in Christian MindFullness,* second edition. Watford: Instant Apostle, 2014.

Lambert, Shaun. *Flat Earth Unroofed: a tale of mind lore.* Watford: Instant Apostle, 2013.

Langer, E. *The Power of Mindful Learning.* Addison-Wesley Publishing Co Inc, 1997.

Lawrence, Louise, J. *Sense and Stigma in the Gospels: Depictions of Sensory-Disabled Characters.* Oxford: Oxford University Press, 2013.

Louth, Andrew. 'Evagrius on Prayer', in *Stand up to Godwards: Essays in Mystical and Monastic Theology in Honour of the Reverend John Clark on his Sixty-fifth Birthday.* Edited by James Hogg. Salzburg: University of Salzburg, 2002.

McCown, D., D. Reibel and M. S. Micozzi, *Teaching Mindfulness.* New York: Springer, 2011.

McGrath, Alister E. *The Open Secret: A New Vision for Natural Theology.* Oxford: Blackwell Publishing, 2008.

Malbon, E. S. *In the Company of Jesus: Characters in Mark's Gospel.* Louisville: Westminster John Knox Press, 2000.

Marcus, Joel. *Mark 1-8: Anchor Bible.* New York: Doubleday, 2000.

Marcus, Joel. *Mark 8-16: Anchor Bible* New York: Doubleday, 2009.

Marshall, Christopher D. *Faith as a Theme in Mark's Narrative.* Cambridge: Cambridge University Press, 1989.

Palmer, G. E. H., P. Sherrard and K. Ware (eds.), *The Philokalia.* London: Faber & Faber, 1979.

Sabin, Marie Noonan. *Reopening the Word: Reading Mark as Theology in the Context of Early Judaism.* Oxford: Oxford University Press, 2002.

Segal, Zindel V., J. Mark G. Williams and John D. Teasdale, *Mindfulness-Based Cognitive Therapy for Depression.* New York: Guilford Press, 2002.

Sheldrake, Philip (ed.). *The New SCM Dictionary of Christian Spirituality.* SCM Press, 2005.

Siegel, Daniel J. *The Mindful Brain.* New York: W.W. Norton & Company, 2007.

Siegel, Daniel J. *The Mindful Therapist.* New York: W. W. Norton & Company, 2010.

Spidlik, Tomas. *The Spirituality of the Christian East.* Translated by Anthony P. Githiel. Collegeville, Minnesota: Liturgical Press, 1986.

Stiegler, Bernard. *Taking Care of Youth and the Generations.* Stanford, California: Stanford University Press, 2010.

Watts, Rikki E. *Isaiah's New Exodus in Mark.* Grand Rapids, Michigan: Baker Academic, 1997.

Wax, Ruby. *Sane New World*. London: Hodder & Stoughton, 2013.

Williams, J. Mark G. and Jon Kabat-Zinn (eds.). *Mindfulness: Diverse Perspectives on its Meaning, Origins, and Applications*. London: Routledge, 2013.

Williams, M., & D. Penman, *Mindfulness: A Practical Guide to Finding Peace in a Frantic World*. Piatkus, 2011.

Witherington III, Ben. *Jesus the Sage: The Pilgrimage of Wisdom*. Edinburgh: T & T Clark, 1994.

Witherington III, Ben. *Jesus the Seer: The Progress of Prophecy*. Minneapolis: Fortress Press, 2014.

Journals

Current Directions in Psychological Science

Emotion

Interpretation

Journal of Clinical Psychology

Journal of Spiritual Formation & Soul Care

Journal for the Study of the New Testament

Sociological Theory

Zygon

Websites[175]

http://www.goldhillholidays.co.uk/
http://mindandsoul.info/

---

[175] All accessed 16th November 2015.

http://www.worthabbey.net/
http://shaunlambert.co.uk/
http://shaunlambert.co.uk/podcasts/
http://flatearthunroofed.com/

The podcasts that accompany this book were produced by Wiseword, a Christian media services and production agency that provides a range of bespoke television and radio solutions predominantly for the church and not-for-profit sectors. For further details, contact Gary Dell on gary@wiseword.tv.

We hope you enjoy the following taster of these books, which are also by Shaun Lambert:

Flat Earth Unroofed: a tale of mind lore
Instant Apostle Fiction, ISBN 978-1-909728-05-9, RRP £7.99

A Book of Sparks: A Study in Christian Mindfullness (second edition)
Instant Apostle, ISBN 978-1-909728-15-8, RRP £9.99

Flat Earth Unroofed
a tale of mind lore

Shaun Lambert

The post-apocalyptic Land of Ge is ruled by a cruel despot with dark and mysterious powers. He is prepared to ravage the land and even sacrifice his own daughter, Mimne, to stay in power.

All that stands between Mimne and certain death is her friend Hudor with his mind lore and timecraft. Pursued by her father, further apocalypse threatens as dark creatures long foretold emerge from the mists of time to stalk the land.

And yet, it is not only evil that is stirring...

Instant Apostle Fiction, ISBN 978-1-909728-05-9, RRP £7.99

Chapter 1
Hudor
and the Palimpsest of Bentley Wood

So it began here, with a forgetting of colour, the colour of flight. It began with the woodpecker dead on the grass in the back garden beneath the apple tree, its wings nailed to the ground, the wind ripping them apart. No more would grass grow under where it lay. He did not know whether this death was aimed at him, whether it was a random act of cruelty, or whether it was aimed at all of nature. Green and red feathers were dimmed by death, no more a laughing call, or swooping flight, or the prediction of rain. That was only the first sign. Storm.

The white hare danced, boxing outside his window. He knew it could not be so. He was in a waking dream, a dream so real it was as though the hare was fighting an invisible foe, and white fur tinged with blood flew in the air. In the dream awake he saw the ordinary street, cracked pavements, tarmac road, grass verge, houses and gateways begin to dissolve, and a nothingness was there. But in the ordinariness he saw gold shining, and he knew it was the end of all things. He got up at once to run but a voice said, 'Write and draw what you watch, where you walk, in your lane and beyond as far as you can. Watch and write and draw what you capture on water-marked paper. For that will preserve the warp of your world against that which comes, and those who come. Watch those who make a weakening of the self, for they are walking. Learn to hide your whole self.'

As he awoke, he felt an emptiness and an aching loss within his heart and he knew that he had heard true. Outside his window was the apple tree, the dead patch in the grass, and beyond that the high wire fence to the school field. But it was quiet outside. It was not a school day.

He dressed quickly and went outside into the front garden. By the road, against the hedge, a white hare trembled. It did not resist his hands, and it was like a knowing from his dream that he was to put her – for the eyes told him it was a female – in his satchel. The eyes looked human. He thought he saw an old man dressed in black on the corner of the road – the man with the scarred, marred face who lived in Bentley Wood. But when he looked again there was no one there. He felt irrationally guilty and wondered if he had been seen, but all that was there was a robin on the rubbish bin.

Everywhere there were people who worked for the Fowler. The Fowler had recently banned parents from teaching their own children. Every child now had to go to a controlled school.

He began to walk along the road on his way to Bentley Wood. The Wood had other names but these had been defaced. He thought he might release the hare there. As he turned the corner of the lane, he jumped. The old man was there looking at him. He found it hard to look at his face, but the eyes were kindly.

'Need to learn how to hide yourself, I reckon,' said the old man. Part of him wanted to stop and ask him why he said that, but he kept on walking, giving him a surprised sideways look as he went.

'Go to Friend's Meadow,' said the old man quietly. And then he was gone.

He always felt better amongst the ancient woodland. Friend's Meadow felt too close to the approach road and the houses so he went further into the woods. He followed the meadow that ran between the two sections of woodland, as if he was following an invisible line on the ground. He was being pulled to the left and to the top of this ancient piece of land.

Suddenly he could sense the rich smell of cow dung. The ghost cattle had been in this part recently. They were called ghost cattle because they had the ability to appear suddenly without being noticed.

He felt he should stop at the spring that bubbled up into a shallow pond. He knew for a moment that he was safe and not being watched. He knelt down and carefully took the white hare out of his bag. The hare looked at him calmly. He carefully washed the blood out of its fur, but there seemed to be no wound; it was as if the water had healed the wound.

The hare watched him with onyx eyes. Out of the corner of his eye he saw two other hares appear, watching him. He was still. He noticed that the cut on his thumb had gone when he had put it in the water.

He knew the hare had wanted him to see this. He could not explain it to himself, but he felt in that moment as if he knew something, as if he knew they were ancient watchers. In watching, they were guarding something, something they had shown him. And then they were gone.

He knew it was time to go home. It wasn't good to linger and draw attention to this place. He went home via a different route, picking up conkers as he walked to give himself a reason for being out.

As he walked home he thought about the old man. Mac, he was known as. Hudor knew that he worked in Bentley Wood below the big house. The big house was where the Master lived – the Fowler as the locals called him. Hudor was allowed in the Wood, which had open spaces and meadows and lakes, although it wasn't open – it was all fenced off. He was allowed in because his dad worked the guard dogs in the Wood. The old man, Mac, also helped with the dogs. He felt he should talk to Mac. He was excited about the white hares, but he didn't want to think about the woodpecker.

Hudor wished he were invisible. He could imagine his skin peeling off him if he were to be caught in the gaze of the Fowler.

He was where he shouldn't be, walking as stealthily as he could. He could hear his breathing and see his breath in the early morning frosty air. Suddenly somebody laughed, and he nearly jumped out of his shoes.

He looked around. A bird with a red crown and a green body walked round a tree trunk and out of sight. Hudor could see nothing else.

Hudor walked on; he needed to get to the top of the hill. Suddenly the green bird with the red crown undulated past him. It had a yellow rump. He heard the laugh again. It was the bird. The bird landed on the tree. 'Yaffle, yaffle,' it laughed.

As the bird laughed for the third time, Hudor was suddenly aware of black clouds gathering, faster than he had ever seen before. He needed to be quick.

It was then that the bird spoke. He would remember that moment for the rest of his life. As the clouds seemed to speed up, time around him seemed to slow down.

It was an oracle. He knew that now, but he didn't know it then. 'Follow the scryer to the path of the seed and the underwritten sentence or your soul lose…'

The bird turned its head and long beak to one side and looked at him with golden eyes and black pupils. Suddenly the eyes blazed with a light that left him with a longing in his heart for he knew not what.

And then it was gone. A green woodpecker! he thought. He didn't know there were any left. And one had died in his garden.

He was by now on top of the hill. In his vision it was a dark night, and there was no light pollution, only a clear sky streaming with starlight. Silence was all he could hear. His heart strummed with joy and his mind was as clear as the sky.

He was floating just a foot above the ground, pale clothed. He could see in front of him an open book. It was out of reach, but he knew he must find it in real life.

His eyes felt suddenly bright with light, and he could see that underwriting lay faintly on the upturned page. Overwriting in a different language and pen could also be seen.

He felt as though he was part of nature, his body humming with the music of every particle. But he also sensed a counter-vibration, something wrong, a storm coming. As he watched the sky, the moon began to turn red.

He remembered it all as if it were yesterday. Then he was back in this dimension, trying to get home without being seen, ordinary daylight all around him.

At supper he asked his father about Mac.

'Old Macarius?' said his Dad. 'Not all who wander are lost.'

This didn't help much, thought Hudor. He knew his dad liked to give short riddling answers, often from ancient books that had been lost.

'Yes, old Mac,' said Hudor.

'He's one of the last peregrini,' said his father. Hudor didn't like to ask more, but he didn't think calling him a falcon was particularly illuminating.

'Have a chat with him,' added his Dad, unexpectedly. Ask him to show you some of his — woodcraft.

'I will,' said Hudor, and he did.

A Book of Sparks

A Study in Christian Mind*Full*ness
Second edition

'Do not conform any longer to the pattern of this world, but be transformed by the renewing of your mind.' (Romans 12:2)

In this second edition of *A Book of Sparks*, Shaun Lambert offers an extended introduction into the universal human capacity for attention and awareness, known in the world of psychology as 'mindfulness'.

Shaun shows how biblical awareness and attention overlaps with secular mindfulness, and has distinctives. Transformation comes through what Shaun calls 'mind*Full*ness' – the practice of being filled with the awareness of the presence of God.

This new edition contains a more detailed introduction and a thought-provoking, practical study guide. It enables us to go deeper on our spiritual journey of transformation through a 40-day study examining the watchfulness modelled by Jesus in Mark's gospel. The writer demonstrates how God can transform us as we develop our own watchfulness, and highlights key contemplative practices such as the Jesus Prayer and *Lectio Divina*. It is an invitation to mindful reading and living.

Instant Apostle, ISBN 978-1-909728-15-8, RRP £9.99

Day 19: The distortion of ecoalienation

Place is very important in Mark's gospel – the desert, the mountain, the sea. The mountain is the place of epiphany and encounter with God. Every time I spend time in the mountains I can feel myself coming alive physically, spiritually and emotionally, in a way that doesn't happen in everyday suburban life.

I've been privileged to visit the mountains regularly as chaplain for a group organised by fellow Baptist Clive Beattie who runs Gold Hill Holidays – a Christian outdoor activities ministry.

I have a sense that this periodic awakening is deeply significant. One aspect that contributes to it is the ethos of the holidays, which is not 'hotel Christianity', but more 'muscular Christianity'. The group travels out by coach, with the food and equipment required for a week in the mountains. An 18-hour coach journey requires patience and fortitude, but also helps bond the group in a way that flying wouldn't. Everyone has to help on one day of the week in preparation and serving of the meals.

The phrase 'muscular Christianity' was coined in 1857 in a review of a book by Thomas Hughes (1822–1896), author of *Tom Brown's Schooldays*, who was a strong advocate of the link between sport, exercise and the development of Christian character. Charles Kingsley (1819–1875) was another Victorian advocate of muscular Christianity, with an emphasis on pursuits such as fishing, hunting and camping. Implicit in this is the benefit of spending time in God's creation.

The strand I would like to tease out is the benefit of spending time in God's creation. My own experience of coming alive in mountains suggests there is something very important missing in suburban life.

One of the possibilities is what the late Howard Clinebell, pioneer of pastoral counselling, would call 'ecoalienation'. In a book called *Ecotherapy* he argues that ecoalienation happens to all human beings when we lose our connectedness with nature.[176] This is an idea which has theological merit and deserves further exploration from a Christian perspective.

This ecoalienation often goes unrecognised without the corresponding experience of ecobonding, like mine on the mountains.

The other common experience reported by people is, 'I feel closer to God in the mountains.' Mountains touch on our deeper alienation from God.

My concern with all of this is that ecoalienation is built into our Western consumerist culture.

One of the very helpful things I have seen in this one small ministry is the number of younger leaders that the founder Clive Beattie has encouraged and developed over the last 20 years.

It is not just our own physical, spiritual and emotional health that is at stake, though. Howard Clinebell argues that 'the most serious, most dangerous health challenge all of us in the human family face is to reverse the planet's continuing ecological deterioration.'[177]

In the mountains at times I have been made very aware of the fragility of the earth's ecosystem, with a shortage of snow, and unseasonal temperatures threatening the famous downhill skiing race in Wengen, known as the Lauberhorn.

Stanley Grenz points out in his book *Theology For the Community of God* that part of God's plan for us as the community of God's people is to live in harmony with all of

---

[176] Howard Clinebell, *Ecotherapy: Healing Ourselves, Healing the Earth* (London: The Haworth Press, 1996), 26.
[177] Clinebell, *Ecotherapy*, 1.

creation.[178] Another important insight he outlines is that sin never just affects us alone; sin is our failure to live in community with God, with each other, and with the natural environment. What we also rediscover in our engagement with the natural world is our own embodiment; we come to our senses.

Our ecoalienation sleepwalks us towards an uncertain future. It is only an awakening of our connectedness to the earth that will enable us to navigate that future. For as Howard Clinebell puts it, 'our children will ask the world of us'.[179] But can we give it to them? One of the distortions is that we often don't even see that we are suffering from ecoalienation, or the part we are playing in the ecological crisis.

---

[178] Stanley J. Grenz, *Theology for the Community of God* (Carlisle: Paternoster Press, 1994).
[179] Clinebell, *Ecotherapy*, xi.